GOLD THUNDER

GOLD THUNDER

Autobiography of a NASCAR Champion

by Rex White
as told to Anne B. Jones

with a foreword by
Rick Minter

McFarland & Company, Inc., Publishers
Jefferson, North Carolina, and London

Photographs are from the Rex White collection
unless otherwise credited

LIBRARY OF CONGRESS ONLINE CATALOG DATA
White, Rex, 1930–
Gold thunder : autobiography of a NASCAR champion / by Rex White
as told to Anne B. Jones ; with a foreword by Rick Minter.
p.   cm.
Includes index.
ISBN 0-7864-1975-X (illustrated case binding : 50# alkaline paper) ∞
2004018784

British Library cataloguing data are available

On the cover: *(top)* Rex White, 1960 championship season;
(bottom) White and his number 4 Chevrolet, Daytona, 1963
(both photographs courtesy of Motorsports Images and Archives)

Manufactured in the United States of America

*McFarland & Company, Inc., Publishers
Box 611, Jefferson, North Carolina 28640
www.mcfarlandpub.com*

To Frankie Schneider, Bill Steel, and Louie Clements.
They helped make my racing career possible,
and successful. True motor-sports professionals,
they were also my friends.—R.W.

Acknowledgments

As Anne Jones explains it, writing is like building a race car. You build a good chassis, add parts, listen to the sound of the engine, fine-tune it, and see how it holds on the track. We hope this book holds your interest, and brings you as much joy as we found in writing it.

We are grateful to all of those who have helped us in this project, and ask forgiveness of those who find errors. We did the best we could researching, and confirming facts and chronology, but the best of intentions are paved with potholes, and at my age, my mind has some gaps.

We are indebted to Motorsports Images and Archives for the use of some photographs reproduced in this book.

We also owe thanks to Nancy Kendrick, Motorsports Images and Archives; Betty Carlan, The International Motorsports Hall of Fame in Talladega, Alabama; Ed Clark, Atlanta Motor Speedway; Dale Snyder at Snyder Video Productions, which houses The Bruce Craig Video Archives (www.SnyderVideo.com); Frank Stark, Raceway Ministries; Doug Allen, Motorsport America; "Captain" Herb Emory, WSB Radio; Harold Reeves, Living Legends of Auto Racing; Larry Hinson, Rick Minter, the Rev. Bill Brannon, Sidney Jones, Eddie Samples, Mike Bell, Jimmy Mosteller, Bob Moore and all the members of the Georgia Automobile Racing Hall of Fame, who helped to make the publication of our manuscript possible.

To express our gratitude to everyone involved would take more pages than the book, but we would especially like to thank Anna Collins, Ned Jarrett, Marvin Panch, Junior Johnson, Greg Fielden, Gerald Hodges, Alex Gabbard, Louise Smith, Ivan Stephens, Sonny "Satch" Steel, Harlow Reynolds, Larry Jendras, Jr., Allan Hall, Richard Sowers, Ronnie and Bobbie Sanders, Jack Turner, "Butch" Nixon, ThunderRoad USA, Charles "Slick" Owens, and Charlie Bagwell. — R.W.

Table of Contents

Table of Contents

Foreword

In his farewell column in the *Atlanta Journal*, the great sports editor Ed Danforth wrote about a lesson his father had taught him years before. He said his father told him that when courting the young ladies it was best to "pick a time when you're both laughing, then get your hat and leave."

Those words, written decades ago, are still good advice for young suitors, for newspaper writers and for race drivers.

Rex White, who may or may not have read Mr. Danforth, was at the top of the sport when he pulled off the track for the final time—an exit that came while he and his fans were still smiling about his on-track accomplishments.

Sure, he was a bit peeved at NASCAR and General Motors for their lack of support, and there may have been other reasons, but nevertheless, Rex drove off into the sunset before the time came when he couldn't win anymore, before he needed special favors like past champion's provisionals just to get in races.

The way he performed in his era, the way he left the sport, and the way he was able to build another life outside racing, make him forever a winner, forever a champion, forever a hero.

Rick Minter
Sports Writer
Atlanta Journal and Constitution

Preface

In the 1950s, Chevrolet racing fans prayed for a savior. *Varoom!* Rex White answered. A little guy, he took on drivers with big-bucks sponsors and powerful muscle cars. Many who met Rex considered him an underdog. That view changed quickly as, pole after pole and win after win, he proved his toughness. Soon, he had become a role model, overcoming a little-known but debilitating physical handicap, helping other drivers who were struggling, and developing a knack for innovation.

Refusing to be bullied on or off the tracks, Rex White became known for endurance, consistency, and speed through corners. Within ten years, he had entered 233 races, with 28 wins, 66 races led, 110 top fives, 163 top tens, 36 poles, and 4,583 laps led, with over 40,000 laps and over 36,000 miles completed. He had become one of the winningest drivers in NASCAR history.

In 1960, he won the Grand National (Winston Cup) Championship, the Most Popular Driver Award, and the Stock Car Driver of the Year Award. In 1961, he received Motor Life's 1961 "Man of the Year" Award. During 1962, he shocked racing participants and fans by winning the coveted 1962 Atlanta Dixie 400 with a 409 engine.

Famous for his eye-catching gold and white Chevrolet known as "Gold Thunder," Rex White was the first to use weighted jack screws and is credited with developing chassis designs that are still used today. He is also known for nurturing other drivers and being kind to fans.

Rex White is listed by NASCAR as one of its Top Fifty Greatest Drivers. A two-time driver for Chevrolet, he is a recipient of the Living Legends of Auto Racing Pioneer Racing Award and the Smokey Yunick Pioneer Award. He is a member of the National Motorsports Press Association Hall of Fame at Darlington and the Georgia Automobile Racing Hall of Fame.

Rex White disappeared from racing for many years, leading to much speculation and mystery over his whereabouts.

Gold Thunder tells the story of Rex, the man in the gold car. In this book Rex shares with brutal honesty the hardness of his mountain childhood, his courage in overcoming polio, and his determination, despite all odds, to become a champion.

When I first met Rex White, it was in the least expected of settings. My husband Sidney and I attend a tiny church in Riverdale, Georgia. Located not far from Atlanta Motor Speedway, Fellowship Baptist has an eclectic congregation. It draws many race fans and participants because its pastor, Bill Brannon, is a chaplain in Raceway Ministries.

I had been working on a thriller novel, and my thoughts that Sunday morning were probably as much on that as they were on Bill's sermon. As we were about to leave, Sidney nudged me and pointed to a slight, unassuming man in the back pew.

"That's Rex White!" he announced with the reverence I might have reserved for a president. "If you want to write a book, he's who you should write about." That said, he took me by the arm and led me to Rex.

Today, my husband refuses to accept any credit for bringing the book to life, claiming the "Gods of Thunder" would not rest until the book was written. Bill Brannon, who had been a Rex White fan nearly all of his life, was among the first to encourage the effort, despite Rex's modest protests. Bill immediately began putting me in touch with motorsport professionals and organizations who would prove helpful.

The outpouring of support for Rex's memoir was astounding. Groups such as the Georgia Automobile Racing Hall of Fame and Daytona's Living Legends of Auto Racing began sharing stories of Rex and the early days of what they called "real racing."

As historians, writers, drivers, and other celebrities extended their help, I realized Rex White was as loved for his generosity as he was admired for his racetrack success. As we slowly began our work, we developed trust in each other, and a wonderful friendship began.

As I met with him day after day, I was fascinated by the complexity of the personality I saw emerging. Far removed from the glitz and glamour associated with racing today, Rex had doggedly fought his way to championship at the same time he was helping others, even those competing against him.

Rex's Spartanburg garage was a hangout for new drivers wanting to learn and older ones needing help. He gave parts to black driver Wendell Scott, loaned an engine to Johnny Allen, helped soon-to-be greats such as Tiny Lund and gave money to rival Marvin Porter when he was too broke to feed his family.

Pop Eargle designed his lifesaving fuel check valve in Rex's garage, using Rex's tools. All of this was at a time when Rex was struggling himself, barely making ends meet, spending night after night working on his car, traveling from racetrack to racetrack, running sometimes twice a week.

In working with Rex, I discovered an honest southern gentleman, modest about his accomplishments, too polite to refuse my requests for continuing interviews. Two thousand working hours later, the book is complete, and I feel I know Rex as well as I know my brother.

Rex grew up during the Depression in the poverty-ridden mountains of North Carolina, where his friends were the sons of moonshiners and mill-workers. Although he claims to have only a third grade education, I found him wise, and as knowledgeable about physics and aerodynamics as a Georgia Tech graduate.

The tales he told brought me sometimes to laughter, sometimes to tears. We had fun writing this book, approaching it as if planning a race. Many a day we'd work to exhaustion, then throw up our hands and go out for Dos Equis. We planned our strategy over chips and salsa at the neighborhood Mexican restaurant.

Gradually, as if I'd boarded a time machine, Rex led me on a journey into the early days of racing. Another world, it was one in which men were judged not by their status but by their ability, and hard work's reward was pursuit of their passion.

Striving for excellence, drivers risked all they had, including their lives, to follow their hearts. Lacking money and modern tools, they ran on shoestring budgets, doing nearly all the work on their cars, beating and banging out parts from junkyard castoffs.

I soon realized Rex's story was not only about himself, but about a brotherhood. Bonded through the trials and tribulations of the track, drivers were dependent on each other for survival. A mobile racing community, they celebrated each other's wins, and held each other up during times of despair. Many remember Rex with special fondness; their comments, quoted in this book, come from personal interviews in which they eagerly shared their memories.

Rex's book became a story of and for all of them, as he shared their frustrations and disappointments along with their joys. It is a lesson in courage, in overcoming adversity, and in realizing one's dreams.

I hope you will like the book. I know you will like Rex. He is an unforgettable and amazing man who has powerfully influenced my life.—A.B.J.

"Racing has taught me how to rationalize things, how to figure out solutions to problems. If you devote enough effort, you'll be a winner, whether you're running a warehouse, or a Chevrolet."

Rex White
1960 NASCAR Champion
and Most Popular Driver
Member of NASCAR's Top 50 Driving Legends

1

Carolina Moonshine Country

"I admired Rex as a race driver because he was a little guy. I started out small, graduating from high school at 5' 4" and 110 pounds. Seeing him winning encouraged me to chase my dream."
—BOBBY ALLISON (1983 Winston Cup Champion, 1964 & 1965 Modified Champion, Six Times Driver of the Year, Member of NASCAR's Top Fifty Drivers)

At eight years old, working on my parents' Model T, I had no idea the skills I was learning would change my life. I was unaware the car on which I labored represented hope to people around me, frustration to those trying to stop illegal moonshine. I saw automobiles as transportation, not the symbol of an upcoming billion-dollar sport.

I didn't know how to tear down fences to reveal new worlds, or how to use simple life principles to propel myself on the fast track to winning. I never imagined I'd become a racing champion.

Back then my imagination was fueled by what I saw around me, and a burning desire to escape. I viewed life through the eyes of a child, and saw it as demanding and hard.

Later, I realized that anyone can be great if they have a good teacher, and the classroom can be found outside of school. Mountain boys' classrooms were the land and their souped-up cars, and knowledge of both was essential for their survival.

Most teenage drivers adapted their skills for quick mountain turns and modified cars to run at high speed. They were a source of pride to boys racing through the valley to impress their girlfriends. At that age, fish and deer held my interest longer than girls, whom I still don't understand. I didn't know loving them could bring you joy, or wreck your dreams.

My dreams were often interrupted by my father's wake-up call or the screech of tires. At night, I'd lie in bed listening as liquor-laden cars sped by. Coming down the road outside our farm, they'd round curves so fast, I thought they'd come through the walls. I'd hear their sound in the distance start as a hum and grow to a roar, a throbbing rolling thunder, echoing through the hills and piercing the night.

I was born in Taylorsville, North Carolina, during the poverty-ridden time of the Depression. Our town, nestled in the foothills of the Brushy Mountains, is part of Alexander County. The land, in the western Appalachian Highlands, is characterized by rolling topography, and bordered on the south by the Catawba River. Its population was less than 2,000.

In the mid-twentieth century, those desperate for survival began our country's first illegal drug trade, running booze. The enterprise wasn't new. Our nation was founded on illegality and revolution, both rumrunners and slave traders taking part. Products with heavy taxation were exchanged duty-free in secret, brought in by boat or any other means one could find for their transportation.

Booze runners, or transporters, as they were called, ran illegal moonshine. Working stills had gone on for generations, but in the early twentieth century, the government's attempts at taxation put legal production in the hands of a few. Small-time producers found their livelihoods threatened. They answered that threat with a roar of rebellion heard throughout the peaks and valleys of the rugged southeast. To them it was an issue of states' rights, and they resented the government for making them criminals when they'd been freely producing booze for a hundred years.

The four things producers needed were corn or rye meal, water, sugar, and fire. No matter how tightly sugar was rationed during the war, they always had enough to make their whiskey. With their biggest challenge the hiding of smoke, bootleggers tended their stills in the cover of darkness, with only the moon to light their way. They usually hid them deep in the woods or in mountain caves close to streams and had to constantly watch them. Moonshiners worked hard, chopping and sawing wood for their fires, and they were constantly hauling, bringing in bags of ingredients, then taking their product out. They carried their whiskey on horse-pulled sleds or wagons and loaded it onto cars to be taken to customers.

Some would take their loads home where they'd hide jars wherever they could, sometimes in the barn or under haystacks. Their families followed strict codes of privacy. Tight-lipped and protective of their property, they kept to themselves and had few friends.

Cars thundered down from the mountains carrying loads of "white lightning," sometimes flavored with fruit, and so strong it could take your breath away. Drivers changed to heavy springs to hold bigger loads and became skilled at evading the law. They used part of their profits to soup up their cars, keeping one step ahead of police, and sometimes each other. Ingenious at engineering and aerodynamics, they soon outdid the efforts of major automakers, some of their cars reaching speeds of 150 miles per hour. It wasn't unusual for drivers to double their investments, making several runs a night and taking in hundreds of dollars per run.

Due to mountain folks' competitive nature, they were soon bragging about whose car was fastest and trying to outrun each other. Several would come together for a demonstration and the thrill of racing spread.

The first races were held on highways, but as groups of cars competed, they needed more space. "Agriculture racing," as it was called in the South, was held in fields, dirt lots and pastures. The cows were shooed away, stakes were laid out in a quarter-mile circle, and hay bales were used as guardrails. Audiences gathered to share the excitement, and organized racing began.

Seizing the opportunity for money-making, promoters sponsored events, charged admission and awarded cash prizes. With reckless disregard for safety, they allowed crowds to mingle with drivers, and sometimes managed to leave without paying the purse.

The wild and unruly spectators staged contests of their own, turning verbal disagreements into drunken brawls. Using their cars as grandstands, they sat on hoods and perched on roofs for a better view.

Woods were used for restrooms and streams for bathing. Food often consisted of Moon Pies with RC Colas. If drivers needed tools, they begged, borrowed or made their own, using anything handy. Tire irons were used on cars, and for communication, providing an easy means of attitude adjustment. If that didn't work, the next tool might be a knife or a gun.

You "run what you brung," with little or no regulation, no matter what condition it was in. Racetrack bullies attempted to establish their territory and bumped trespassers out of their way. Races were constantly restarted to haul away crashed or broken down cars. Women sometimes raced, usually as a gimmick to draw attention. Fights, wrecks, and trips to the hospital were considered part of the show. It would be years before the sport was brought under control with the formation of NASCAR.

The earliest racing site to become well known wasn't a pasture, but a beach that became famous for confusion and chaos. Daytona's wide sandy shoreline made a perfect track. When cars went out of control, instead of hitting a tree, they spun into the ocean, if, by the grace of God they didn't veer into spectators.

The first Daytona race was between Ransom E. Olds and Alexander Winton in 1902. They tied, with a top speed of 57 miles per hour, only about a fourth the speed of drivers at Daytona today. The next year Winton won a multi-car race topping 68 miles per hour, a big event, as no one had ever driven over a one-minute mile.

From that day on, speed records were just numbers to be broken, and Daytona drivers were usually the ones to do it. Most ran as close as they could to the water, where the beach was harder, some running with their wheels in the ebbing tide. Their attempts were a source of onlookers' entertainment, as cars sank in the sand, or sped into the sea.

Barney Oldfield, the country's first racing hero, reached over 83 miles per hour at Daytona, in America's first eight-cylinder engine. His race car, made from two four-cylinder engines bolted together, was a sight to behold.

As speed increased, excitement increased, and those early contests drew attention to cars and the growing automobile industry.

Interest in cars grew to a fever, along with interest in their performance. In 1909, the Indianapolis Motor Speedway was built on a large tract of farmland northwest of Indianapolis, Indiana. Planned as a testing facility for the automobile industry, it soon became the site for racing competitions. Car manufacturers wanted to impress spectators, because they were customers, and winning cars meant an increase in sales.

The races were so successful that they eventually evolved into the world-famous Indianapolis 500. Held annually, for years it was the speedway's only race, and it still draws hundreds of thousands of fans. The track set an auto-racing standard for others to follow and decades later, many of its ideas were copied at the Daytona International Speedway.

In 1927, Major H. O. D. Seagrave, from England, reached 200 miles per hour at Daytona in his Golden Arrow streamliner. He wore racing's first safety helmet, made of leather. Drivers often used aviator caps to keep hair from their eyes, fleece-lined waterproof caps, and motorcycle or football helmets.

English driver Sir Malcolm Campbell was attracted by the feats of the beach drivers and decided to show off his skills at Daytona in his "Bluebird." He reached 300 miles per hour, shocking the world. The news of such speed was startling, but it would be a long time before I knew of it.

Others knew, and for years they rode the beach's "Flying Mile," testing how fast they could go in their high-performance cars. They'd have a mile to get up their speed and a mile in the trap. For a small fee, they were officially timed by NASCAR on the same clock used by the race drivers.

Daytona, Atlanta, and Charlotte were the main hot spots for racing, with Charlotte the most inventive. In the early twenties, a wooden speedway with an adjoining wooden grandstand was built. The track was a quarter-mile oval constructed of two-by-fours laid on edge. Unfortunately, the track was short-lived, due to termite infestation and weathering.

During the hard times of the thirties, a man named Bill France left Washington, D.C., with his family and settled in Daytona. He'd worked in a garage and having been a driver, decided to race again. After working several jobs he opened an Amoco station, and began overseeing races on the Daytona Beach and Road Course.

Some say the first stock car race was held there in 1936. The races were a mess, especially for those trying to score them. Drivers were constantly getting stuck or breaking down, and were helped back into the race by the crowd. Wrecks were so exciting, they became a main feature, and spectator interest grew. Other people's interest was growing too, especially back in the mountains.

Like any mountain boy's childhood, mine was difficult. My family relied on themselves. There were fields to plant, firewood to chop, and livestock to feed. Some people believe we survived on luck, but if we did, we created our own. My Dad believed in working from can to can't: "from mornin' when you can till dark when you can't." He said, "Hard work ain't never killed nobody. You make your own luck." Each child was to earn his keep. I was doing chores by the time I was six, and was self-reliant from an early age.

You've got to use your head, and a lot of it's discipline. My father taught me, "If a thing's worth doin', it's worth doin' right." If you did something he didn't like, he'd whop you as hard as he'd whop a mule.

One thing he didn't like was not working fast; another was not being perfect. I can't count the times I was "slapped side the head," or my face got punched.

"Ain't nothin' wrong with makin' a mistake," he often said, "but being stupid is a different thing."

Something he didn't have was sympathy. "Never say I can't do that. Say I'll try, then do it." He taught me if something bad happened, you put that out of your mind. You done turned that page over. Don't talk about what's behind you; say what you're gonna do.

I can hear his voice as he pulled his old denim jacket over his overalls, buttoning it against the chill of winter mornings.

"C'mon boy," he'd call, his expression a look of fierce determination.

I've seen him come back with that coat wet and frozen, so stiff it would stand on the floor. I had one just like it I called my "overall coat."

11

On our farm, my mother, my sister Mae Lynn, and me. "There were fields to plant, firewood to chop, and livestock to feed."

We never stayed in due to weather. Snow and ice just meant more hurry in checking and feeding the animals.

An unexpected last child, I was the runt of the family, but my father didn't allow for my smallness. He expected big things. As short as I am, I'm taller than he was. When he got mad, he'd remind me, "You're lucky to be here."

The things we used to accomplish amaze me. One of my chores was to sit on the churn and crank it to make our butter. I have that old churn and treasure it.

My mother's ability to adapt to such a hard life was astounding. Basing our meals on the outcome of crops, she had to plan them a year in advance. At three a day, that was over a thousand for five hungry people.

She worked hard her entire life, rarely leaving the county in which she was raised. Having little in the way of luxury, she didn't wear makeup or have time to primp. She wore her hair long, caught up in a bun and held tight with hairpins. She never spent money just for herself. She was still chopping wood to fuel the fireplace in her nineties.

Numbed by the toughness of life, she showed little emotion. Working from the time she got up in the morning until time for bed, she raised chickens from biddies and did all the work in the gardens except the plowing. I saw her many an afternoon, wearing brogan shoes, hunched over a hoe. Making

Left: My mother, Arlie White. "She worked hard her entire life, rarely leaving the county in which she was raised." *Right:* My father, Wade M. White. "My Dad believed in working from can to can't, from mornin' when you can till dark when you can't."

soap in a black washpot over a fire outside the house, she used Red Devil Lye you can buy in the grocery and homemade lard.

A Christian woman, she spent her relaxation time reading the Bible. More educated than most of the women I knew, she taught me as much as she could about day-to-day living. She made sheets, blankets, curtains, and most of our clothes. Mother loved to sew, and quilting was her favorite pastime. Seated in a straight-back chair, she held the fabric tight on a wooden frame, moving its boards to adjust the width. She used scraps of the cloth flour sacks left over from aprons and dresses. Back then, the sack cloth's pattern helped a flour brand to sell. I have one of those quilts, and still use it on cold southern nights. It reminds me of how she sacrificed for our family.

During the day, there was a constant background of kitchen noise, the sizzle of meat and clanking of spoons in cast iron skillets. We could tell what she was fixing by its smell and looked forward to southern fried chicken and homemade bread. She canned beef, cured hams, and ground sausage, saving the fat to make lard.

Sometimes, we cooked in the fireplace, baking Irish and sweet potatoes in its ashes. Thankful to have enough food, we never thought about diet. We could make a meal out of cornbread and milk, and I still remember my Dad boiling roots for tea.

The only thing we didn't grow was pinto beans, and I've seen him buy a hundred pound sack of them for the winter. My father didn't want help, so as not to be indebted, and had his own blacksmith shop that stands on the farm today.

I was forced to focus on work because he didn't believe in play, and kids weren't thought of as children, they were laborers. Whenever I had time to think, it was always about getting away, especially to my secret place on the river. I'd paddle the boat he helped me build, bailing out water to keep it from sinking, then park it under a cave. I'd have to remove the snakes, but it was my favorite spot, and out of the rain. I'd sit there for hours, watching the smoke and smelling the mash from liquor stills.

Having brought potatoes, and corn with shucks, I would pack them in mud, and roast them in a campfire. When they were done I'd crack the mud, pull off the shucks, and that was good eating. I'd learned to swim by tying an oil can around my waist and I could stay there and fish for two or three days.

I wasn't allowed to have fun, no entertainment, and rarely a film. When I could, I'd sneak down the road to town, spending nine cents on a movie and a penny for an all-day sucker. I'd get a tongue lashing from my father, but the thrill was worth it.

It was hard to get money back then. We had little cash, but there were no bills. Before electricity, we used kerosene lamps. We paid up front for all we bought, never having heard of a charge card. I trapped rabbits and sold peaches, watermelons, and milk, earning what I could, delivering the milk by horseback or wagon.

I hated farm work, felt like I was being driven just like the mules. I know now it's good for life to be hard, at least growing up. If it's too easy, you don't amount to anything. Vowing as a youth to get away from that farm, I wanted to be outside its fences. I guess in my mind, if I was going to be driven, I'd do the driving.

I stayed tiny because I'd barely eat, still drinking milk from a bottle until the first grade. I'd squirt the cow's milk into that bottle, then take it into the closet and hide because I was embarrassed. When I entered school, I was still a runt, and ran right into a bully. He was bigger, but I was determined not to get walked on. When he began picking on me, I jumped him and won the fight, learning that size and power weren't important if you had good strategy.

I was a mischievous child for sure, always testing the limits, seeing how far I could go. Curiosity was killing me, but I didn't like school, hated all my teachers, except Mrs. Davis. I liked Mrs. Davis because she never rode your back, but nobody ran over Mrs. Davis. Nothing got past her. If you did something she didn't like, she'd twist your ear, or rap your hands with a ruler. Back then, since education could involve your mind and your backside, there weren't many discipline problems.

I was kicked out of first grade because there were too many kids for the room, and was thrown out of second for goofing off. Both classes were in the same room in our little schoolhouse.

Learning came easy, but I had no use for books. When I didn't go to school, my Dad backed me. He marked his name with a lopsided "X." I don't think he'd ever been inside a schoolhouse, but he could walk up to a tree, put his arms around it, and tell you how much lumber would come from it. He calculated the birth of horses and cows with numbers on the side of our barn. Watching how he studied things would later prove useful to me.

Burning with energy, I wanted to explore the world, and learn about everything. I packed my bags several times, but didn't get out of Taylorsville. When I was seven, I sold apples by the side of the road, made $20.00, and rode with my cousin to Washington. I stayed two weeks and came back with $8.00. When I was nine, I ran away with a carnival, but it was too cold and I had to sleep on the ground.

My real school was the farm. I didn't know it then, but I know it now. Most of the lessons I learned have stayed with me all of my life. The biggest one was how to conquer fear.

Some people say a race driver has to have nerve. I say he can't have fear. He has to have knowledge and confidence. At 200 miles an hour and over, you have to know what you're doing and feel good about it. If you're afraid of speed, or hitting the wall, you don't need to do it.

I'm not afraid of anything. I'll do anything. If there's something unknown, I'll find out what it is and won't be afraid. An example is snakes.

Before we got our new house, we lived in an old one, with rafters and no ceilings. It was like camping outside, with its cracks in the floors. I used to sleep with my brothers and sisters, all in one bed.

One morning we looked up and saw a snake hanging down from a board right over our heads. The others were scared, but it didn't bother me.

We used to catch fish under rocks by feeling for them with our hands. I once caught a cottonmouth snake, but just let him go. Another time I crawled out of a gulley onto a copperhead. I just rose off the snake and kept going. There are lots of things that can suddenly bite you. If you worry about them all, you won't have a life.

My biggest chore on the farm was plowing the fields. Walking behind the mules, I learned perseverance. They weren't as fast as tractors, and as far as I was concerned, they were too slow. One walked in the furrow just plowed and the other walked the new ground. They'd do over what you showed them, but couldn't think in advance. I'd find a groove, set my pace, and follow along. I learned if I'd hang in, and be consistent, I'd get the job done. That was good strategy then and it held true in life, especially on the race track.

Also being our farm repairman, if something broke, I'd fix it, not waiting for somebody else. I liked to figure things out and know how they worked, what made them stop, and what made them go.

Fascinated by speed, I was always trying to make something go faster, the horse, the buggy, the washing machine. I'd run our horses, chasing "Indians," but mine wasn't the only chasing going on. With white lightning produced in record amounts, revenuers kept moonshiners flying through mountain roads at breakneck speeds.

2

Growing Up

A Life Filled with Deadlines and Speed

"I've always considered Rex a very close friend and have a deep respect for his ability. He was an inspiration to me, and a short-track whiz."
—NED JARRETT (Former ESPN Sportscaster, NASCAR Champion 1961 & 1965)

The first time I really drove I was on our farm, in a 1928 Chevrolet truck. I'll never forget the feeling of power, a tiny kid moving an object weighing thousands of pounds. Until the time came I was constantly daydreaming about how driving would be.

My father bought that truck but never drove it because of its clutch so my brother took it to town, but it was mine on the farm.

The same time I was imagining myself as a driver, others had bigger dreams. Interest in racing was growing. Bill France's promotional talent kept Daytona a hot spot, and there was racing on Utah's Bonneville Salt Flats.

A large salt deposit left by the receding waters of ancient Lake Bonneville, the Salt Flats covers 159 square miles. Similar to beach sand, its surface is hard with a lake at its end. Tested as a racetrack in 1912, it became famous for speed trials. During the forties, fifties and sixties, it was considered a western "Daytona."

During World War II, the nation put auto racing on hold, but nothing was on hold in Taylorsville. The screeching of tires never slowed. Funded by their profits, moonshiners' cars were their biggest investments. The more power they had, the less chance their owners would be caught and jailed. Engines were kept running smoothly and reached higher speeds. Former bootlegger and NASCAR driver Junior Johnson claims moonshine runs gave drivers a jump-start on racing.

Transporters, also called trippers, learned to stay on course, hold tight through curves, and develop split-second reactions and, since police cars didn't have radios, if they could outrun them they didn't get caught.

Of course, not all transporting was done at night or at breakneck speed. Some of the most successful runs weren't run at all. They were slowly driven deliveries disguised as loads of timber or other goods. Police never did make a big dent in "shining." The thing that finally ended it was a rise in the price of ingredients.

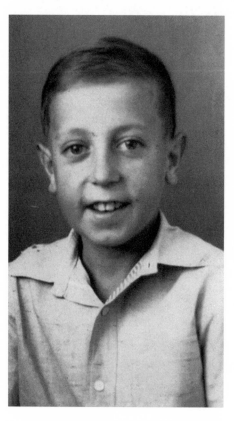

"The first time I really drove was on our farm, in a 1928 Chevrolet truck. I'll never forget the feeling of power, a tiny kid moving an object weighing thousands of pounds."

At the tracks, with competition between cars, and drivers, fan loyalty was fierce. Contests were still held on "make-do" courses but as the sport grew more popular, profits increased. Chaos ruled. Carousing drunken spectators continued to bring danger to the track and it wasn't unusual for drivers to line up to race, only to find there was no prize money. The ticket fees had been stolen and the thief had fled.

In 1947, Ed Samples was voted the finest driver in the United States, but racing was out of control. Deciding something must be done, Bill France invited the most influential car owners, drivers, and promoters to Daytona Beach.

Beginning on December 14th, at the Streamline Hotel, their meeting lasted three days. As they debated the future of racing, France put forth his ideas, proposing a national regulatory organization and a national series. He suggested steps for increasing track safety, insuring fair treatment of drivers and promotion.

Impressed, the group voted him President and formed a Board of Directors. Members included Buddy Shuman, Marshall Teague, Red Byron, and Red Vogt.

One of the most successful early drivers, Ed Samples (left) was voted the finest driver in the United States in 1947. He continued to race for many years. Here he is shown receiving a trophy for the 1949 National Modified Championship from Sam Nunis (center) and Joe Epton. (Photograph courtesy Bruce Craig Racing Photo Archives.)

Vogt, who was Raymond Parks' popular mechanic, recommended the National Association for Stock Car Auto Racing as a name, and NASCAR was born.

Alcohol was present from the start. It was the reason for stock car racing's beginnings, having its roots in illegal transport and consumer demand. Even in bad times, people squeezed out money for booze.

Back home, the tax-paid liquor came out of Charlotte for our whole county. It was surprising how much people would drink. You could buy a pint for $1.25. Moonshine sold for a dollar a pint or three dollars a half-gallon. Most people preferred that liquor to store-bought and, twenty-five cents was a lot. You could put twenty-five cases in a "Forty Ford" coupe for a pretty good load. With only a front seat, its trunk was huge. The car had a powerful V-8 engine and was readily available. Its grille whistled at high speed and you could hear it coming. The car was favored by the bootleggers and the racers. Often one and the same, transporters would make a midnight moonshine run, tape on a number and race the next day.

On the farm, I was involved in a race of my own, trying to finish my chores with time left for play. Still small, I was beginning to develop my arms hauling firewood. Mama was cooking on a woodstove and my job was keeping the tinderbox supplied and cleaning out ashes. It took cords and cords of wood, split and dried, to cook three meals a day. In summer the kitchen was scorching, but full of good smells.

Before refrigerators, we had an icebox. The iceman brought a big block of ice twice a week. In summertime, it'd melt right away, so we kept milk and butter in a concrete trough, pouring in well-water to keep it fresh, and sometimes putting in a watermelon.

Mama was always working, cooking and canning, making pickles or ketchup, baking, or shelling peas. We didn't have bacon like today. We had midlins cut from the bellies of the hogs we raised. That's where bacon comes from, the lower part of the stomach of hogs.

She'd cook ribs, slice tenderloins, and cut meat in chunks to can. We grew sugarcane for molasses, and took our corn to the mill to grind. They gave us flour in exchange for the wheat we grew. We ate sitting in straight-back chairs at a kitchen table my father's ancestors had made.

We only had a few seasonings, mainly salt, pepper, sugar, and saltpeter. Salt was an important preservative and a saltpeter marinade made pork taste better. Mama bought vanilla every few months, when the Watkins man came. Having compassion for those with less, she took in an aunt for several years and made meals for hungry people who came to our door. Being down on your luck and out of a job was common in those days.

We lived by a cotton mill village, called Millersville. Kids there ate food from the company store and had peanut butter and crackers. Their fathers were enslaved to that store by the bills they owed, with little hope of ever fully paying them. Our favorite snacks were Moon Pies and a pop drink named Cheerwine. Sometimes we'd trade lunches, as they liked my ham biscuits. If one of us had what another one needed, we'd pool our resources.

My best friend was a Milltown boy, Nom Eisenhower. By his family's standards, we must have seemed rich. He rarely wore shoes, and had fewer things to play with than I did. Mill work was difficult and demanding. One step up from coal miners, workers earned ten cents an hour, eight hours a day, five days a week. Occasionally, my Dad would hire a mill-worker to help him, and pay him a dollar a day, for which the worker was grateful.

20

The old White homestead at Taylorsville, North Carolina.

Sometimes, dogs wandered over from the village, chasing our animals or eating their food. We kept some of those dogs, but my mother would drown them in the creek, rather than see them starve. We named one black and white mutt Sambo. A mix of Labrador and Collie, rather than be a pest, he worked on the farm. He earned his keep like the rest of us, bringing the cows home at night and herding each to its stall.

The saddest day of my childhood was when he died, killed by a tree my brother felled cutting timber. I feel guilty to this day because as the tree was about to fall, I had called him. I hid my tears, dug a hole, and buried him in our pasture.

In the summers, I looked forward to fruit and berries. Wild muscadine was good for jam or wine. We had grapevines, and fruit trees, but the best were the blackberries Mama made into pies. During our chores, we'd take breaks to eat tomatoes right off the vine, and since I was always hauling and lifting, my body grew strong.

Of all things in life, I loved the rivers best, especially for hunting and fishing. My father let me shoot a twelve-gauge shotgun. It knocked me to the ground the first time I fired it, and I still remember where that happened in

21

the field by the cotton mill. The next time I fired it I held it firmly under control.

Since there were no organized sports, we didn't have football, or play much baseball at school. Our games back then were catching snakes and bullfrogs, or pitching horseshoes.

Children found things to do for themselves, not expecting others to provide entertainment. We'd get an old tire to roll as we walked, or we'd make slingshots and bows and arrows. "Squirt" guns were discovered while milking cows. I'd grab a nipple, take aim at my brother, and squeeze. At school, we used to play marbles at recess. I had two steel shooters of which I was proud, and the competition was fierce. It took a combination of skill and coordination.

I used my muscles to my advantage, trying to outdo other farm boys, playing to win. We'd get into wrestling matches or I'd try to out-swim them. I broke Nom's leg in one of our scuffles. Clifford Fox gave me my comeuppance by pushing my face in a pile of manure. After that experience, there was nothing worse to dread. We loved to fight but, we'd soon get over it, and within hours were friends again.

We stayed close to the farm because of the work. It might be a month before we'd go five miles to town. It took fifteen to twenty minutes in our Model T, but with the wagon and horses, you lost the whole day.

Time was set by the animals, and if we didn't work fast, my father's patience grew thin. He'd kick me in the butt, hit me over the head with a slop bucket, or knock the dickens out of me, if I was dallying. We were always arguing, and once he chased me with a twenty-two rifle when I continued to stand my ground. Farming was about deadlines, just like racing, and speed was a way of life.

My father, with our dog Sambo, who earned his keep like the rest of us, bringing the cows home at night and herding each to its stall.

22

The first thing I raced for fun was an old wagon. I had a couple I'd run off the bank behind our house or our church's steep hill. Nom and I'd attach wheels to a homemade wooden axle, add a seat, tie a rope to the wheels for steering, and be ready to roll. When we didn't have a rope, we'd use our feet. We modified it several times before getting it right.

If you could see that hill we raced on! It was steep enough to slide down, if you had something to ride on, and you'd glide across a great open field.

We learned to race a little Red Flyer wagon. Steering with its tongue, we'd try to stay on the path, avoiding the trees. There was a highway on the hill with a radical turn. I watched automobiles come down it sideways, running wide open. Inspired, I ran off every hill in Millersville, copying the cars.

I also liked horse racing. Nom had an old mule, but I had a good horse. Mules work better than horses, but Toppy could outrun him easily. In looking back, maybe that was my calling. I was small enough to be a jockey, and all you had to do was hop on and ride; but I'd seen a lot of horses from the back, and I didn't know how much money you could make from it.

When I finally got a bicycle, I went flying through the woods and the roads, hunched down and ducking the wind. I was already applying principles of aerodynamics and it gave me a feeling of freedom and power.

We didn't worry about our clothes, and mine stayed ragged. We were always dirty from farming, and it seemed like I was born in overalls. They weren't out of place because everyone wore them. My Dad had one old suit. I didn't see him in it until he was buried. Looking back, I think he should've been buried in his overalls.

I never saw my Father in church, his funeral was held by the graveside; but, every Sunday, Mama insisted

My father Wade White (left) and his cousins Earnest and Charlie.

23

we children go. To make sure I went, she made me church janitor. I rang the bell to summon the members, swept the floor, and built fires in the stove in winter. I kept Sears and Roebuck catalogs in the outhouse.

In the early days, there was no toilet paper. I don't recall my Mom or Dad ever buying it. A piece of paper was a rare thing. That's why Sears and Roebuck catalogs were so popular. We used catalogs or magazines until we got an inside toilet.

When my Dad ran corn through the sheller, it pulled the kernels off and left the cobs soft. He'd put them in a bucket in a corner of the outhouse. Sometimes we used the cobs left over from horse feed.

There were red cobs and white cobs. You used the red cobs first, then the white cobs to check. In the fields, we used leaves, praying they weren't poison oak or poison ivy.

By the fields were acres and acres of timber. We inherited a steam-powered tractor from my grandparents, with wheels eight feet high, and a box to build a fire in. Instead of using it as a plow, we used it to pull our sawmill, making what we needed out of what we had. When we got a newer tractor, the mules had to pull it to start it.

I was still walking behind mules to plow fields when I was ten. By the time I turned eleven, I was falling, my right leg buckling beneath me. Grabbing onto the plow didn't steady me. My father, having no empathy, thought I was avoiding chores as usual. I got several bad whippings before being hurt falling down stairs. It was then he knew something was wrong.

My parents usually served as our doctors, armed with castor oil and kerosene. Kerosene was for cuts and castor oil was for constipation. A good cleaning out was considered a cure for all ills, including the "dickens." When I was bad, my mama threatened to get that "dickens" out, armed with that oil. Some people had aspirin, but even that comes from willow bark. The Raleigh man came every few weeks bringing Hadacol, a tonic for everything from snakebite to rheumatism.

Raised in a time of home remedies, sometimes I felt my cures were worse than diseases. In those days, medicine often came from the yard or woods, but my falling was beyond homemade help. When they took me to the doctor, he said I had infantile paralysis, better known as polio.

The nearest center for treatment was in Gastonia. I visited that hospital twice, seeing hundreds of people whose bodies were mangled and paralyzed. Many were dying and there was no cure. The disease left me with a withered right leg, but I felt lucky to only be crippled and fortunate to be alive. I was fitted with a special brace and shoe. My Dad didn't cut any slack, and I was soon back working the fields.

24

Not long after, I noticed a spot on my Dad's denim coat rubbed thread-bare, torn by his shaking right hand. He was diagnosed with "shaking palsy," now known as Parkinson's. As the jacket grew more worn, it symbolized his life, wearing out, and worn down, from the disease. By this time, my older brothers and sisters had left and I took on more chores.

I liked anything mechanical, finding things I didn't know about, and taking them apart and fixing them. When we got cars on the farm, I repaired them, always having to improvise, especially with tools. We used to jack up a wheel so one tire was off the ground, to make cranking the engine easier. If someone was spinning the back tire, it started more quickly.

I knew that car inside out, using what I had to work with, and serving as a tool myself. My hand was so small I could reach inside the transmission. In winter, since there was no antifreeze, we drained the water at night, to keep the radiator from freezing. We didn't start that car every day, just when we went to town, warming the engine with water we heated in the wash-pot. In the summer, it wasn't bad, but in winter, without a heater, that car was cold.

Sometimes I'd sit in our old Model T, playing with the steering and pressing the pedals, while my mind would run wild. Once I left the emergency brake off and the car rolled down the bank and dented the fender. I got my worst ever whipping, but I loved being in a vehicle, "driving" or riding.

I mastered speed on my horse, and the highway was next. My friends were into racing as much as I was and some of them, as young as twelve, had their own cars. Every time we got together we went fast. The fad was going around corners, especially Dagenhart Curve. The guy I ran with took turns wide-open in an old Model A.

A fellow named Conrad drove a Harley Davidson motorcycle that had a sound of its own. He rode it while wearing goggles and a cloth helmet that snapped under his chin. When he'd rev it, the power of its unmuffled engine thrilled my soul. I knew instantly when Conrad was coming, hearing the roar from miles away.

Guys who had cars met in town at the pool hall, where they'd start running their mouths, boasting about their engines and how fast they'd go. Soon, they'd head for the roads. There was an old, barely used dirt road behind my house. I'd ride in friends' cars as they ran up and down it, sliding through the corners sideways. The first time I was in a car that flipped over, I was riding with another farm boy on that road. We got out and turned the car right side up and off we sped. A four-door Model A, its roof was dented and its doors never closed well again.

Tires were always in awful shape and hard to get. They'd blow out; we'd get out, patch them and get back in.

Although I wasn't into bootlegging, I loved to ride in the liquor cars. Modified with Edelbrock cylinder heads and three carburetors, their engines were stroked and their bores were bigger. We'd run Taylorsville's only red light, aggravating the town's one policeman who worked all the shifts.

"Sledge," as he was called, didn't do much chasing, believing in "live and let live." Not as laid-back, the cop in a nearby county ended up dead. Local cops were generally friendly and the troopers, in their silver and black forty Fords, rarely caused any problems. The Feds, who were looking for transporters, were the ones to be feared.

My most exciting rides were with a friend, hauling liquor from Charlotte. I was around so many stills, I could set one up. You could find them easily enough, always near water. If you followed a creek, you'd soon be aware of the odor. "Shiners" would try to hide them, but usually fail. They put them in chicken houses and pigpens, hoping the stench would cover the smell, but the hens and swine ate the mash and walked around drunk.

Mountain folks used to tell tales about revenuers and stills, how they'd always try to trick people into taking them to them.

An agent would tell a kid he'd give him $2.00 to take him to his Daddy's still. The child would take him in the woods and ask for the money. When the agent complained they weren't there yet, the child would tell him he had to give him the money because the agent wasn't going to make it back out.

A guy rode into North Wilkesboro and asked a man on the street where he could buy some moonshine. The man pointed to the Post Office and told the man that was the only place he couldn't buy it.

The maddest I've ever seen my Dad was when I got into liquor, not hauling, but trying to make it. Nom and I had a liking for the home brew made by his father, and decided we'd make some wine. We mixed ten pounds of sugar with muscadine grapes. That sugar had been bought for Mama's canning.

Dad made and kept white lightning, but rarely drank it, preferring to give it away. He liked a shot of apricot brandy when he was cold, saying it would heat you down to your toes. He never got drunk or used tobacco. Most men chewed while their women dipped snuff. When Nom and I wanted a drink, we'd go to the Silver Moon, a roadhouse that sold booze, despite our dry county. Bootleggers went there to shoot the breeze and play pool. Everyone got served, regardless of age. It was the first place I drank beer out of a bottle.

My family bought a plug-in Philco radio and thought it made us modern. We loved Lum and Abner, and listening to Amos and Andy. Nom and I also had a liking for the Grand 'Ol Opry, and I enjoy country music today. My favorite song is "El Paso," sung by race driver Marty Robbins whom I raced with at Nashville in '65.

Listening was about all my father could do. As the Parkinson's progressed, his speech became slurred; his walking slowed, and he could no longer care for the farm. His shaking increased, and his jacket wore all the way through.

Defeated, he reluctantly agreed to move to a house in town. He worsened with every passing day, the life draining out of him. Today, when I see a man in a worn denim jacket, I think of my dad.

As soon as I was old enough, I got a job hauling chickens for our grocer, Scott Stamey. I also hauled half-gallon fruit jars to people who said they were canning, but, I knew what they were doing. Nobody needed fifteen cases of fruit jars to can. They might buy a couple, or even five, but most people didn't can in half-gallons. They canned in quarts. Some customers ordered fifteen cases, then in two weeks ordered fifteen again. This happened in the winter when there were no crops.

The railroad brought boxcars full of fruit jars for our little town. They were a job to unload by hand into a truck, and again from the truck to the warehouse. It took days with a little pushcart loaded with five cases at a time. We sometimes received such large orders, we delivered them straight to private homes.

When I wasn't working, I turned my attention to my friends' fast cars and a girl named Mary Lou. There wasn't much to do, so our dates were just meeting downtown and watching movies.

I couldn't wait to get away from Taylorsville. At fifteen, I stole three of my Mama's chickens to sell, and then a buddy and I headed to Washington. We hitchhiked for three days, making it to Pennsylvania Avenue with fifteen cents in our pockets. When the money ran out, we didn't call home; we just got jobs.

Each of us had a park bench for a bed near the Calvary Street Bridge, a spooky area over a gorge, known for suicides. We both worked at the Toddle House, washing dishes on different shifts. He worked during the day and I worked at night. Our food was free while we were on duty, so we'd eat enough to last us until the next day. It was there I ate my first waffle, covered in butter and syrup.

Our first paycheck went for renting a room and buying clothes. In our hurry to get out of Taylorsville, we hadn't brought a suitcase, or anything else.

It wasn't long before I became friends with the customers. One was Bob Wright, who told me he was never wrong. He'd order coffee and doctor it with booze. He and his wife had turned their home into a rooming house and it wasn't long before I was a tenant. My new roommate was another Toddle House worker from Taylorsville, named Larry Milstead. We made good money at twenty-five cents an hour, paying five dollars each, weekly, for our room.

27

Climbing the corporate ladder, I became a whiz as a short-order cook, serving food quickly, making shift quotas. Things were going well, until I sliced my hand with the bread knife, learning speed is not so good when using sharp objects.

I worked at several restaurants, but always went back to the Toddle House. It was while I was working there that I pursued my new hobbies. Cars and girls had become my main interests. I liked to tear down motors when they broke, fix them, and put them back together. My life came together, too, when I met a girl named Edith Byrd. Good looking and five years older than me, she soon won my heart.

At the end of the war, Ford began shipping chrome bumpers to customers to replace their wooden ones, and new cars rolled off assembly lines. Although production was a priority, it took time, and it would be months before dealerships could meet consumer demand. My brother-in-law was high on the waiting list because he was a policeman. When he finally got a car for $800, he immediately sold it for a thousand, making a profit.

A lot of people had hand-me-down cars. When they got new ones, they just parked their old ones in their backyards. They didn't lose their worth then, like they do today. Some held or increased their value for fifteen years. You could always get a good deal if you had cash money.

With the war ended, racing's hiatus ended too, turning attention to the souped-up stock cars, still running the southern mountains.

3

Motorsports Mania
Another Magical World

"I loved to hear the engines. You'd hear a roar when they first cranked up, and everybody would stand. Hot dogs always seemed better with the taste of grit and sweat mixed in, and, oh yeah, I enjoyed the burnt rubber smell. When you got ready to leave you'd have soot all over you."

CHARLES LANGFORD (Race Driver and Fan)

Raymond Parks had his start in the moonshine business at the age of 18. He drove a '26 T Model Ford Roadster hauling 60 gallons a night. He later raced, but found he made more money as a car owner. He was known for having the best driving teams in the country and backing Bill France. When France first got started, he'd promote races, then participate in the events driving Raymond's car. Raymond hired top mechanics such as Red Vogt. Vogt got into racing while working for Parks by souping up bootleggers' cars.

In February of 1948, just months after NASCAR began, the first sanctioned modified event was held. Atlanta driver Red Byron won on the Daytona Beach and Road Course. Many of the drivers would soon be famous, including Tim, Fonty and Bob Flock, and Marshall Teague; but Byron, in a Raymond Parks' Oldsmobile, was a standout. He had racing expertise and toughness, and his car had been tuned by Vogt.

A former World War II tail gunner, Byron had had his left leg smashed by Japanese anti-aircraft fire, requiring him to wear a steel brace attached to his shoe. He also had a modified clutch pedal. The Vogt-Parks combination dominated early NASCAR racing, especially Daytona. Their cars looked good

29

Top: Driver Fonty Flock would become famous. *Bottom:* Red Byron was a stand-out. He had racing expertise and toughness and his car had been tuned by Red Vogt. (Both photographs courtesy Bruce Craig Racing Photo Archives.)

Raymond Parks (left) with Rex White in 2002. Mr. Parks still attends racing functions and likes to reminisce about old times. (Courtesy Anne Jones Photo Collection.)

and ran well, and propelled Byron to a National Championship that year. Vogt eventually mentored well-known car builders Ray Fox and Smokey Yunick.

Gober Sosebee ran a 1947 street Buick during one of the Daytona Modified events. According to his son Brian, Sosebee was one of the first people to drive a stock car on a NASCAR course. The car caught Bill France's eye, contributing to his future interest in stock car racing.

Gober was also the first known driver to repair a car with cow dung. Once, when he was at Georgia's Peach Bowl, he ran into another driver and knocked a hole in his radiator. There was a stockyard next to the track so Gober quickly climbed over the fence, grabbed a handful of manure, plugged the hole, and won the race.

Another time, he was racing in Lithonia, Georgia when he went off the fourth turn, rolled down the embankment, then came up the access road and continued the race.

Unaware of these events, I was charting my own course and married Edith. We'd honeymooned in Taylorsville, where she met my parents, and I'd taken a job pumping gas and working on cars in Maryland.

Left: Red Byron won the first sanctioned modified NASCAR event in 1948 on the Daytona Beach and Road Course. *Right:* Fonty Flock at Langhorne in 1948. (Both photographs courtesy Bruce Craig Racing Photo Archives.)

In 1949, Bill France held an exhibition NASCAR event at Broward Speedway, near Miami, a five lap, ten-mile race. It was won by a local driver, Benny Georgeson, who was driving a Buick. The first Modified race was held at North Wilkesboro and the first Strictly Stocks at Charlotte Speedway.

NASCAR never barred women or minorities. If you had a car and a pit pass, you could race. The Charlotte race included Sara Christian, who ran six strictly stock races that year. She placed fifth in one of them, at Heidelberg, Pennsylvania. Her finish remains the only female top five finish in NASCAR today.

With a purse of $5,000 at stake, Bob Flock sat on the pole, but sidelined by engine problems, became Christian's relief driver. The winner at first appeared to be Glenn Dunnaway in a 1947 Ford, but he was disqualified. Jim Roper, who'd driven a '49 Lincoln, was given first place.

The second race of the season was held at Daytona, and included Louise Smith, and the Flock brothers' sister Ethel Mobley. Her brother, Tim, claimed

Jap Brogton, Langhorne, August 15, 1948. (Courtesy Bruce Craig Racing Photo Archives.)

Ethel was named after the gasoline. She loved racing against her brothers, but usually raced in the Atlanta area.

Louise Smith was encouraged to participate in racing to draw publicity, but when she came in third in her first race, people looked at her differently. She's credited with winning thirty-eight modified events in eleven years, competing as far south as Daytona and as far north as Canada. Involved in many spectacular crashes, she took racing seriously and broke almost every bone in her body proving it. She had to be tough and fierce, as many of the drivers resented females encroaching on what they considered their territory. Fortunately, she and her husband owned an auto parts yard. She came to be known as the "First Lady of Racing," and would eventually be voted into the International Motorsports Hall of Fame in Talladega.

There have been many women drivers throughout the years, and there are many female fans, but the sport is still, without question, male-dominated.

An early race in Langhorne, Pennsylvania in 1948. (Courtesy Bruce Craig Racing Photo Archives.)

One of racing's most far-reaching events occurred when team owner Hubert Westmoreland filed a lawsuit against NASCAR over the interpretation of rules, when one of his cars was disqualified. Rumored to be a moonshiner, Westmoreland had run a winning car with altered rear springs, and he sought $10,000 in damages.

The Greensboro, North Carolina judge handling the case refused to intervene and his ruling set a precedent for cases thereafter. NASCAR was, in effect, given the authority to make and enforce its own rules.

By the end of the year, former champion Red Byron was first in Final Point Standings for Strictly Stocks. Lee Petty was second, with Bob Flock third.

I was still pumping gas, helping customers, and repairing their automobiles. I used to volunteer to tear cars apart and fix them, not knowing what I was doing. Somehow, I'd fix them back, to the relief of their owners. One man was so impressed, he hired me to work in a dealership, but the business closed and I went back to the service station.

In Taylorsville, everybody drove Fords. Only old folks drove Chevrolets. When I bought a car, it was a '37 gray humpback Ford coach with a tweed interior. I pulled the heads, changed the carburetor and timing, and had a new engine. Equipped with a new motor, that hot rod would go.

I was good at its repair and kept replacement parts with me, having learned to make changes fast. Once, when the car broke down in a funeral procession, I jumped out, put on a new fuel pump, and held our place in line. I kept my car

Fonty Flock receiving congratulations from up-and-coming driver Fireball Roberts (left) and Bill Blair (right) at an early race at Langhorne. Fonty came in first, Bill Blair, second, and Fireball, third. (Courtesy Bruce Craig Racing Photo Archives.)

spotless, cleaning it on the outside and beneath the hood, and was constantly washing it. I even painted the engine.

On weekends, I'd drive Edith to Glen Echo. An amusement park, it had a roller coaster, but its main attraction was an air blower that blew dresses of unsuspecting women over their heads. Occasionally, we'd go to a drive-in movie, especially if it was a western.

I ran everywhere wide open, posting speeding tickets over my dash, and terrifying riders with hair-raising turns. What I was doing illegally on the streets was legal on the tracks, and NASCAR continued to grow.

In 1950 the "Strictly Stock" division was renamed "Grand National," adding a touch of class. It would be the early seventies before its name was changed again, to "Winston Cup," when R.J. Reynolds Tobacco Company became a sponsor. In the summer of 2003, the sponsorship switched to Nextel for the 2004 season.

35

Rex White with Louise Smith at the 2002 Moonshine Festival in Dawsonville, Georgia. "Louise Smith was encouraged to participate in racing to draw publicity. Involved in many spectacular crashes, she took racing seriously and broke almost every bone in her body proving it." (Photograph from the Anne Jones Photo Collection.)

Although it was becoming more accepted, the sport was still firmly tied to its moonshine roots. One tale has been handed down for generations. As the story goes, a bootlegger hauled a load of liquor to Atlanta the night before an outlaw, or unsanctioned race. The next day, with no time to clean out his tank, he entered the race at Lakewood Speedway, and as fate would have it, he won. Before he approached the checkered flag, he saw the sheriff waiting to inspect his car. He signaled for the track's back gate to be opened as he raced past the flag and fled, returning the next week to collect his winnings.

The sport was dominated by Red Byron, Marshall Teague, Curtis Turner, the Flock brothers, and Lee Petty. A lesser-known racer, named Fireball Roberts, had just entered the scene. A former University of Florida baseball player, nicknamed for his fastball, Fireball attracted attention and the press. He would also prove good at attracting owners, mechanics, and rides.

Trying to provide help for drivers, NASCAR offered insurance for competitors and race officials. Northeastern tracks came under the organization's sanction, and the Sportsman division was formed.

When Darlington, the nation's first paved super speedway, was opened, its owner was retired racer Harold Brasington. He had driven the bulldozer that carved out the egg-shaped speedway, and he made history when he paved it. Its shape was partly determined by the preservation of his neighbor's minnow pond, which can still be seen there today.

Its inaugural "Southern 500" was the only 500 mile race besides Indianapolis. The event attracted 75 drivers, and 25,000 fans. The fans loved the new grandstand with its tin roof, although the noise was so loud they couldn't hear well for hours and hours afterwards.

It took six hours for the cars to complete the 400 laps, starting in the morning and lasting until dark. They began lined up three abreast in 25 rows. The most challenging thing for drivers was wearing out tires. Some wore out 50 or more.

The biggest scare of the race was when Buck Baker wrecked, and was declared dead by track officials. Worried about the heat, he'd taken a jug of cold tomato juice with him. When he crashed, the jug broke, sending a gallon of red liquid over his head. The first rescuers to the scene thought he'd been decapitated. Ironically, a former bus driver, he was known for his wisecracks and being comical. Later, he would gain attention for marrying one of Darlington's beauty queens.

Californian Johnny Mantz won the Darlington race, driving a 1950 Plymouth, owned by Hubert Westmoreland. His prize was over $10,000. Impressed, Bill France later recruited him to organize NASCAR's West Coast Division.

At the end of the year, Bill Rexford, a former hot rodder from New York, was the youngest driver to win the National Points Championship, and he did it with only one victory, after Lee Petty and Red Byron were disqualified. They lost their points after driving in non–NASCAR-sanctioned events.

Racing was getting hotter and hotter. I was working at the gas station one day, when a man walked in with a sign for West Lanham Speedway. He asked if he could put it in the window. I looked at that red and yellow sign for weeks, saving my pennies, growing more excited and determined to go. When the time came for the race, Edith and I were seated in the backstretch.

The track was a quarter mile of circular asphalt with wooden grandstands made of boards without backrests, and separate outhouses for men and women. The first car out was number 4F, a '37 Ford coupe, like my coach. My eyes followed that car as it made its first lap. Painted red and black, its side panels

Top: Wally Campbell was considered one of Langhorne's best drivers. *Bottom:* Wally Campbell was later tragically killed in a racing accident, cutting short what could have been an outstanding racing career. (Both photographs courtesy Bruce Craig Racing Photo Archives.)

removed revealing its motor, it held me spellbound. As if seeing a vision before me, I looked at the driver and knew that was what I was going to do.

Race after race, I returned. The good drivers ran at Lanham because they competed against the best such as Wally Campbell, Frankie Schneider, and Charlie Dyer. They ran in Richmond, Virginia, and in New Jersey, two hotbeds of northern racing.

Most guys worked weeknights after their day jobs in garages at home, searching for, or making replacement parts when they could. People with high interest made themselves experts. Tools were hard to come by and folks learned to share. They had no choice but to be dependent on each other.

Frankie Schneider races with #36 Pee Wee Pobletts at Dorsey Speedway in Elkridge, Maryland, 1954. Harry Clifton Photo. (From the Larry Jendras Jr. Photo Collection.)

At the track, I could tell the pros from the amateurs by how they cut corners, and, at that time, they started in the back. Most of the cars were at least ten years old, built in the 1930s or '40s.

It was fun to watch them fight their way to the front. Bumpin' and spinnin', catchin' and passin', the cars made a heck of a show. They ran on methanol alcohol, shooting fire from their exhausts and filling the air with fumes.

I was burning to get in the pits and talk to the drivers, but located outside the infield, they were blocked by an eight-foot fence. Finally, I pried loose a board and let myself in.

I entered another magical world. Men worked furiously as revving engines sent shock waves of noise through the air. I'd never heard such a sound.

Tires and parts were strewn everywhere, and workers walked around, across, and on them. I'd never been close to race cars with their slick tires and modifications. These were set up for asphalt, some with two or three carburetors, and you could tell which fuel they were running by its smell.

Escaping detection, I blended with the crowd, unable to take my eyes off the cars. At first, I rarely spoke to anyone, just mingled with mechanics and drivers, listened and learned. I couldn't see the race, but gave it up for the new world I'd found, and conversations with frequent winner Frankie Schneider.

The start of a 200-mile stock car race at Langhorne, Pennsylvania in 1949. (Courtesy Bruce Craig Racing Photo Archives.)

Soon, I expanded my territory, taking in dirt races in Baltimore and crossing the Chesapeake by boat to races in Delmar. Delmar, a town in Delaware, reminded me of Taylorsville.

A mechanic I had worked with at the Packard dealership had a race car. A '35 Ford Coach, it was jalopy, or beginner class, but he offered to let me run a few laps at Manassas, Virginia. That was the first time I drove a race car, and the only time I drove that one.

By 1951, NASCAR was attracting more fans, adding two more paved tracks and doubling Grand National races. Wanting to make the sport national, rather than regional, Bill France included races in Arizona, California and Michigan. The sport was expanding throughout the country.

Struggling drivers could rarely afford their cars, much less safety equipment. In an effort to attract more competitors, track promoters began having "Helmet Day" races, awarding drivers real racing helmets instead of prize money. The races were common at the Atlanta Peach Bowl, but you could only win one once. Others had to have their chance, so everyone could get a helmet.

Georgia driver Jack Jackson and his buddies built a car for a $125, but he had no helmet and no money to buy one. Since he'd never raced, he'd had no opportunity to win one. What he did have was an old aviator hat with goggles and an air raid helmet, so he got the bright idea of sewing the two together.

During one of his early races, his car flipped over, the force ripping the helmet away. As it rolled across the track, fans panicked, thinking it was his head. When he got out they must have thought he'd come back to life.

One driver did "come back to life," and that was Joe Caspolich. Joe was from Gulfport and raced from Mobile to New Orleans. Once when Joe won a race he gave his trophy to a thirteen-year-old boy who had been hanging around the track. The boy was touched by Joe's gesture and never forgot it.

Years later, Joe was seriously hurt in a race, taken to a hospital and pronounced dead. His wife left his room and Joe was covered with a sheet and wheeled out into the hallway. By that time, the young boy had grown up and was an intern in that same hospital. He saw Joe's name listed as deceased and, grieving for his favorite driver, he went to find Joe and pay his respects. When he saw Joe's body under the sheet on the stretcher, he decided to take a look at him. When he reached down and lifted the sheet, Joe's arm fell out. The stunned doctor quickly realized Joe's heart had started beating again. He rushed him back into the emergency room, where they found he had lots of broken bones, but he was not dead.

Joe's best win was second behind Jim Reed in the Southern 500. He has had some hard breaks in his life, but is a symbol of toughness. When he retired, he returned to the Gulf Coast and decided to remodel his house. He was standing on his roof with a skill saw in his hand when he had a heart attack. As he fell, the saw cut off his hand at the wrist. A medic who lived next door heard him screaming, rushed out, wrapped the hand in a towel and sped Joe to the hospital, where it was reattached.

In the '90s, Joe's wife was killed after a barge hit a railroad bridge outside of Mobile. The impact knocked the track out of line and the Amtrak train she was riding went off the bridge and into the bayou. Joe is still living today, and is a member of the Darlington Unocal Club.

I'm also a member of that club, which was formerly sponsored by Pure Oil, which was bought out by Union Oil, and was involved in NASCAR for over fifty years. Membership is based on having the fastest qualifying time in each make of car.

Daytona, in 1951, was the hub of NASCAR racing and set the pace for change. Marshall Teague won the year's opening Beach and Road Course event, and unbelievably, I was there. Edith's sister, Estelle, wanted to go to

Florida and offered to pay for our vacation, if I would take all of us. We toured the state, ending up, since I was driving, in Daytona, just in time for the race.

The beach and the town were overflowing with fans. We watched in disbelief as we passed race cars running up and down the streets and parked at motels. I wondered why the event was held in February and learned it was the time of the year when the tide was low.

We went to the Modified race on Saturday and the Grand National on Sunday. I saw many drivers I'd seen at West Lanham, and was amazed at the course. The backstretch was on A1A, bordered by houses, and the front stretch was on sand, where I saw cars spinning into the sea.

The noise of the revving engines drowned out the surf as the smell of exhaust mixed with salty air. Drivers came off of pavement onto sand. There were oyster shells, but on the south turn, there was the beach with holes big enough to sink a coupe in. Drivers would hit those holes and go sailing through the air. The best thing they could do was put in good shocks.

Visibility was hard with windshields blasted by sand and salt water. They took the paint right off of the cars. There were sometimes spectacular wrecks, such as Joe Lee Johnson's fourteen flips on the South End Straightaway.

We parked by the pits on the beach and just walked in. The day of the Modified Race, I saw Frankie Schneider, and met his car's owner, John Bolander. It was the first time I'd met an owner and I was impressed.

When Marshall Teague

Marshall Teague (right), shown with an unidentified friend, was considered the "King of the Beach." (Courtesy Bruce Craig Racing Photo Archives.)

won on Sunday in a '51 Hudson Hornet, others were also impressed, particularly the car manufacturer's executives. Seeing a promotional opportunity and seizing it, they decided to give Teague new cars and parts, hoping for a rise in sales. Pure Oil supplied oil and gas. Teague, who had grown up in Daytona, was known as "King of the Beach," and became famous for his Hudson "Teaguemobiles."

Detroit drew attention during a celebration of the city's founding. A race was held with drivers representing five automakers, and many company officers were present. It was war, as the cars slid along the dirt course out of control and into each other, or broke down because of bad parts.

Wanting to see their cars win, manufacturers began targeting their parts and engines for high performance, with the Hudson Hornet being the first to form a racing division. It was headed by the soon-to-be-famous engineer Vince Piggins, who was later hired by Chevrolet. Some of those who benefited were Red Byron, Marshall Teague, Lee Petty, Curtis Turner, and the Flocks. By then they were known throughout the country and had large followings of fans. Herb Thomas, from Olivia, North Carolina, took the Final Point Standings in the Grand National Division.

Despite progress, all was not well with NASCAR. Upset by the rowdy, drunken crowds, dangerous tracks, and gambling, politicians introduced bills to ban the sport. They failed only because of Bill France, who used his political power to stop them.

Back home, I kept going to West Lanham races and sneaking into the pits. Enjoying being with drivers, I decided I'd learn more if I made myself useful. One night, in 1952, Frankie Schneider accepted my help. I did whatever he asked me to do to his maroon and white '39 Ford.

From then on, I headed for the track on Friday evenings to change wheels and tires, and remove his car's axles after the race. Sometimes, he would invite me to eat with his wife, Dolly, and his helper Bo. Occasionally, I'd help him in Baltimore.

Continuing to observe, I watched the different ways cars were set up. The guys who were winning had better springs and shocks and the best cars always had a floater rear end. Reminding me of the liquor cars, race cars firing up became my favorite sound, and the noise still excites me.

4

Racing Fever

Frankie Schneider Becomes My Mentor

"Today it's a corporate affair, a lot of money, a lot of glamour. In the old days, those guys raced!"

DON JOHNSON (Brother of Joe Lee Johnson,
Member of the Johnson Racing Team)

Feeling part of a racing team, I traded my car for a forty Ford coupe that looked like a race car. I loved that forty Ford, and wish I had one today. Cars on the track looked like race cars too. In 1952 NASCAR first required roll bars. The early ones were sometimes made from exhaust pipes. When Tim Flock tried a two-by-four, upset officials made a rule that a roll bar wasn't legal unless a magnet stuck to it. People were always pushing the rules and as soon as they did, NASCAR changed them.

Many automotive-related companies were now taking an interest in racing, and helping drivers who promoted their products. Two of the most prominent were the Pure Oil Company and Champion Spark Plug, Inc. Champion gave extra prize money if you won with their plugs in your engine. Pure Oil supplied gasoline and motor oil products. Red Byron, Lee Petty, Tim Flock, Marshall Teague, Herb Thomas, and Curtis Turner were still big names in racing.

Previously, Bill France had scheduled many conflicting events in order to promote NASCAR's exposure, but he decided to spread out the dates, making it easier for drivers and allowing concentration of the most powerful competitors within single races where their rivalries and battles fueled the public's excitement.

Daytona had problems controlling the crowds, and many people could watch events without having to pay, which ate into racetrack profits.

Darlington was still the only super speedway, and the Southern 500 brought in drivers chasing big money. It also provided radio coverage. Nothing could rival the track's popularity. Overflowing its concrete grandstands, thousands watched from the grass.

Fonty Flock got $9,430 for winning the 1952 race. His brother Tim, who was considered the best of the Flock drivers and later won the Grand National Championship, was famous for his constant companion, Jocko Flocko. Jocko, a pet monkey, rode in Tim's car in a special roll bar cage in the front seat area. His gear included a custom-made harness and racing cap, and he was the hit of the fast-track circuit until tragedy struck. During a Charlotte race, Jocko was able to wriggle out of his harness and stick his head into the hole in the floor used to inspect tires. He must have been hurt by the tire, for he suddenly climbed up on Tim's neck and started screaming. That was Jocko's last ride and he was never the same. Tim's siblings, Bob and Ethel, who were also drivers, inherited their love of speed from their father, who was a bicycle racer. Their other brother, Carl, was said to be a moonshine runner.

Before the end of the season, Frankie's helper, Bo, was drafted into the army. That winter, the Schneiders invited Edith and me to go with them to Florida. Always supportive, Edith agreed. She was willing to do anything to help me follow my dream, and soon, she and Dolly were friends.

We shared the Schneiders' home, and I caught extra jobs when I could, working as a trucker, as a gas station attendant, and on a shrimp boat. We were so broke, I sold my Ford but, Frankie, a balding, opinionated Dutchman, became my mentor.

Frankie was fast in everything he did. The funniest eater I've ever seen, he ate so quickly, he didn't have time to chew. When eating bananas, he left on the peels.

As his mechanic, I learned about bite and stagger, making more or less wedge to go faster through corners. He taught me to set up the car, increase horsepower, and work on a racing engine. He also trained me to select gear ratios and tires, set the chassis, make repairs after wrecks, and adapt the car for each track. We paid attention to every detail because little things could keep you from winning.

I learned how to survive in racing with no money. It was hard to get racing parts in the fifties anyway and since we couldn't buy them, we made our own. All race cars were built with a lot of welding because you had to weld the chassis and make front and rear bumpers. With a torch and electric welder, you could build a good car.

Like other racers, we had a basic toolbox, consisting of a hammer, sockets, wrenches, and pliers. A lug wrench and a jack completed our kit. There weren't markers to write with in those days, so Frankie sometimes used lipstick to draw his number on the side of his car.

Since he raced three to six times a week we stayed busy, but I was hungry to learn. As I worked, my passion for racing grew, turning into obsession. When we went to a race, we went to win and usually did.

Always helping others, Frankie didn't want help for himself. Like my father, he didn't want to be obligated, was stubborn and thrived on problems. He couldn't work in a nice clean shop and liked to be surrounded by junk. In fact, he collected it. Frankie enjoyed working in mud like on a farm, and I've worked with him in mud up to our ankles. The dirtier, the more behind, and the more pressured he was, the better he ran. After we'd worked together awhile, he began to include me in decision-making.

Rushing from track to track, we didn't lose time. He'd begin driving with me asleep in the backseat. Part way, we'd change. I'd slide into the front beside him on the driver's side and put my foot on the throttle as he moved over. We learned to do this at high rates of speed.

Once while we were crossing the Chesapeake Bay on a ferry, we worked on the car, changing the intake manifold. After the ferry arrived, we took the hood off and tied it to the roof with a bungee cord. I sat on the fender with my feet on the frame, and Frankie went on to the track, pulling the car with me on it fixing it.

Frankie loved competition and wanted to beat the other guys by outdriving them, not through better equipment. He believed racing was a psychological thing. If you were up against drivers who had faster cars, you simply outsmarted them. Being with Frankie was like taking a class in Racing 101, and he had more influence than anyone else on my driving career. I still have great admiration for him, and respect.

While we were still in Florida, Frankie was put in charge of another racer's car. He agreed to let me drive it on two dirt tracks in Tampa.

Used to the asphalt raceway at West Lanham, I found those tracks full of dust. I slid sideways most of my first race, and part of the second. The '37 Ford I was driving wasn't set up right. The kingpins were frozen and it wouldn't steer.

I was unable to qualify in the first race feature, but after working on the steering, came in fourth at the second track. That wasn't saying much because there were only four cars. I wasn't racing; I was just hanging in there.

Frankie may have thought that embarrassing experience would satisfy me, but it only served to whet my appetite. His statement that I would never be a race car driver only fueled my fire.

Frankie Schneider at Reading Fairgrounds in 1962. (From the Larry Jendras Jr. Photo Collection.)

Frankie knew what he was doing and won many of the races he entered, although he believed it was better to take second or third than risk getting hurt. He placed fourth at West Palm Beach, 11th at Daytona and third in Jacksonville. We traveled to Columbia Speedway, where he came in fourth. It would be 1957 before he'd win a Grand National race, driving for the Chevrolet factory team on my recommendation.

While I was at Frankie's, one of my visitors was a man I'd met at West Lanham. Unknown to me, he'd been so desperate to drive, he'd stolen a car. Unfamiliar with racing mechanics, he'd chosen a Ford, with a six-cylinder engine. Somehow, he managed to place in the West Palm Beach Grand National before police finally arrested him for car theft at a track the following year.

48

"Frankie Schneider knew what he was doing and won many of the races he entered, although he believed it was better to take second or third, than risk getting hurt." (Courtesy Bruce Craig Racing Photo Archives.)

Meanwhile, Herb Thomas won twelve Grand National races, taking the Final Point Standings again and almost $30,000 in prize money. We returned north with the Schneiders to start the new season.

One of our races was at Langhorne, Pennsylvania. It was a round track without a straightaway; cars coming out of the last turn were running blind. The first car wrecked and others followed. In those days, there weren't any caution flags, and fifty to sixty cars continued to pile. Wally Campbell was in the pits, and one of the cars slammed into his, starting a fire. It was the most awful sight I'd ever seen, but nobody was hurt. Wally got out of his car and ran through the smoke without getting burned, but the memory of those flaming cars stays with me.

I worked with Frankie until midseason in '53, but there was little pay, and he was more demanding than my father, plus he had a short fuse. I hung in as long as I could, before leaving for a job at B&D Welding in Maryland, where I worked in the machine shop and hauled cylinder heads for the railroad. Still driving fast, I once sped down a snow-covered mountain in Hagerstown.

"Frankie loved competition and wanted to beat the other guys by out-driving them, not through better equipment." (Courtesy Bruce Craig Racing Photo Archives.)

There was so much weight on the truck, I had good traction, but a trooper pulled me over. He said he wasn't going to give me a ticket, he was going to give me a trophy!

I'm not one to outrun the police, although I do admit to one incident. I was going 110 miles per hour to Daytona with a 327 engine. A cop got behind me, but since there was nothing in front of me, I let her rip and sped away.

Because of my northern tag, I was thought to be a "Yankee," and was caught for speeding in Ludowici, Georgia. I wasn't driving fast, but I might as well have been. Ludiwici was a speed trap town, surviving on ticket-based tourist revenue. I had to pay a $15 fine, and at the time that $15 meant a lot. It was that little town's revenge for Sherman's "March to the Sea."

"Brownie" Brown, one of B&D's owners, had a red and white '37 Ford I'd seen him race at West Lanham. When the other owner was absent, we worked on the car during company time. Wally Campbell was one of his drivers. Campbell, who also drove for Wally Marks, was a charger. He was later killed in Indiana in a sprint car.

50

My wife had a distant relative I'd met in Florida named Bill Steel. He knew Brownie and was also a race car owner. We were both living in Silver Spring, Maryland, and because of our family relationship, I got to know him. His wife's brother, Ducky, was driving his car, a black and white '39 Ford. Although Ducky had talent, he was more interested in booze. Bill asked if I liked to race, and said if I'd work on his car, I could drive it. I soon took Ducky's place, running quite a few races for practice.

The first few times in Bill's car, I spun out, but got better the more I drove it. One night, I tangled with another driver and flipped it.

Bill, his son Sonny, and I decided to build a better car and work as a team. We struggled for over a year, combing junkyards, getting the parts to put it together. Using as much as we could from the old car, we took a floater rear end from a one-ton truck for the chassis. The only things new were our radiator, the tires, a rebuilt engine, and my helmet.

Bill was a guy who could talk a good game and he was knowledgeable. He couldn't work with his hands, but had good ideas and made a lot of money with jukeboxes and pinball machines. I went to him for advice, but I handled the greasy part.

As for driving, I took care of that. Bill never raced, but drove his personal car with flair, alternating placing his foot on the accelerator, then withdrawing it. You'd suddenly go *whoom...*, then drift to a California stop and go *whoom...* again. He talked while he drove, punctuating his sentences with the brake pedal.

A good friend as well as a partner, Bill was always building me up, giving me confidence. He told me not to sell myself short (no pun intended). I built the car and he became my sponsor.

One of the places we raced was Westport in Baltimore. A former baseball diamond, it had a big grandstand and drew large crowds. The race was well publicized and there were a hundred cars. I ran a hundred-lapper and at the end I thought I was third. When the payoffs were made I was placed seventeenth. That's how I was introduced to racing politics.

Once I was qualifying on a dirt track in Concord and ran really well. The race officials told me I couldn't possibly have run that fast and there must be something wrong with the clock. They made me start over and qualify again.

A later example that stuck in my memory occurred in Chicago at Soldier Field. I qualified first on the pole, but when I got ready to race, the promoter who'd rented the track sent me to the back. He said in his race, the qualifying would be inverted. I refused to invert and left. There must have been 90,000 people at that little track that had been built to seat 100,000.

When outsiders came in on regulars, promoters could make things difficult. If you got ahead, they'd wave the red flag, restarting the race with you going slower. They were harder on independents than on drivers with sponsors, and often changed rules at the drop of a hat. I experienced a lot of their prejudice firsthand and know they ruined a lot of drivers during the season.

By 1953, NASCAR was progressing much faster and gaining publicity. France made a new rule that drivers must pre-enter races or lose their points, so the press could promote their appearances to full advantage. Herb Thomas won almost $29,000 and the Championship, but Curtis Turner won over the press. He became famous for appearing at the tracks in a suit and Cadillac. A playboy, he was known for hosting parties and chasing women.

"Little Joe" Weatherly, a champion Harley-Davidson racer, was a sensation when he tried stock cars, grabbing the crown for the Modified Division. Known as the "Clown Prince of Racing," the short, stocky driver was always pulling pranks using rubber snakes, frogs and other scare tactics. He had a box with a wire over it, and said he had a mongoose inside. He'd ask people if they'd like to see it. When they came over to look, he'd push a button, and a fox tail would fly out, scaring the dickens out of them. One of the most superstitious of the drivers, he shunned anything green on race day, even dollars. He usually wore white pants, saddle oxfords, and gloves. His specialty was running dirt.

Fonty Flock was the "Clown Prince of Grand National," sometimes showing up in Bermuda shorts. Despite being a cutup, he was a serious driver, beloved by fans. He once flipped in a race, then accepted spectators' help rolling the car back over, and managed to win.

Darlington continued to dominate the limelight, adding a "Miss Southern 500" pageant, sponsored by the Darlington Police. The winning drivers kissed the beauty queens.

By spring of 1954, I'd finished building the race car for the Steels. We blew the motor three times before discovering it was built with Kleenex in the oil galley. The guy who built the block didn't use shop towels, and plugged tissue in everywhere. When he replaced the plugs in the engine, he forgot to remove it. Although we'd had high hopes for the season, this cost us a month of racing, but at least I gained experience, taking that engine out and putting it in.

One thing I'd learned from Frankie was when you work on your car, you use your head and feel what the car is doing. He knew his car. If something broke, he had to know why. If there was something about his car he didn't know, he'd tear it apart and find out what it was.

Our car felt good and was running well, although I always took along baling wire for instant repairs. Anything could happen on a racetrack, and we had to be ready. It was a matter of using our wits and anything handy.

Bill and Sonny, nicknamed "Satch," served as my pit crew. Satch, a little guy at twelve, would get out of school and run straight to our garage. He was a picky eater, until he met my mom, when we made our first trip to Taylorsville. I also introduced him to the "Dust Sandwich."

Satch and I had planned to race at Allentown, Pennsylvania. When we got there, the race had been cancelled. Our next event was at Wilmington, Delaware. I had enough gas to get there, but we were flat broke and it was twenty-four hours away. We had money for two "Dust Sandwiches" and two Pepsi Colas. That was two packs of Lance cheese crackers and drinks, eaten on the road. We bought Pepsis because, at that time, they were twelve ounces, while with Coke you got only eight.

Lance has been around a long time. Their Moon Pies and oatmeal cookies were also standards, selling for a nickel apiece. Servings were bigger then, and a Pepsi and a Moon Pie would make a meal.

Bill met us in Wilmington, bringing supper money with him, to Satch's relief, but we found there were many times we'd have "dust sandwiches." Once, when we were on our way to Lanham, we stopped at a diner in Allentown where Satch rushed in and ordered pancakes and sausage, not knowing that meal would take our last dime. Race car drivers invented diets out of necessity.

One of NASCAR's earliest female drivers, Louise Smith, still shares stories about those hard times. She recalls when nobody in racing had money. She once split a "tube steak" three ways, sharing hers with two other drivers, when hot dogs weren't a foot long. She claims they'd often share a Coke, and as small as they were, if you took too big a swallow, you might be killed. We were all thankful when we won enough money to buy something to eat.

One fellow never won a race, but finally won a five-dollar bill. He carried it around with him for a year, until he finally ran out of gas and had to spend it.

Satch, Bill, and I were teased about our junkyard car, but we didn't care. It ran well in Wilmington, and Wall Stadium in Belmar, New Jersey. We hid Satch under blankets when we'd go in the gates, since he was too young to be in the pits.

Wall Stadium was a popular spot for racing, and there were a lot of good drivers there. It had very high banking and you really went fast. You had to run well to compete. I ran with one carburetor against the Modifieds and won some heat races. I liked that track, despite never winning a feature. Bill Steel would get frustrated with me because I'd take the lead, and then be outrun by the Modifieds. But winning third was like winning the feature with that group of cars. We'd sometimes pick up fifty or sixty dollars and on big nights over a hundred.

A lot had to do with your number of carburetors. A Sportsman had one carburetor. A modified had three or four. A Sportsman with one carburetor could place second or third and take home more than the winner.

Starting on a Thursday night, we'd have Friday, Saturday, and Sunday to race again. We slept in my truck, and bathed when we could, in truck stops, under hoses, and in streams. We were struggling just to get by, as were so many others.

Short track driver Woody Moore was almost as poor as we were. In 1953, he went to the "Old Horsetrack" on the river in Hawkinsville, Georgia, where he bought a car for $35. After buying gas for two more dollars, four quarts of oil for one dollar and two hamburgers and two Cokes from his last dollar, he found a rope, tied himself into the car's seat and raced.

He came in nearly last, but he finished. The promoter told him if he came back, he'd better have roll bars. He'd never raced legally before, but he'd out-run the law many times. He'd run his '54 V8 Dodge so fast, the State Patrol would be 25 miles behind. All they had at the time were Flathead Fords.

I ran with the hot dogs, refusing to go where there wasn't good competition. Once when I went to Langhorne Speedway, I took a friend, John, to help me. He wasn't a NASCAR member, and since we didn't have the $25 membership fee and $2 pit pass, I hid him under tires in the back of my truck. I've never heard such hollering as I heard before I let him out.

During a West Lanham race, I flipped and landed the car on its roof. Another car hit me, spinning me down the track upside down. Despite the drama, I only cut a hole through my chin. Edith, who had watched in horror from the stands, insisted I go to the doctor. Adrenalized, I steadfastly refused, not having seen the feature.

After taking the car home, I decided to build a new one, but everything came to a halt with my Father's death. I immediately went to Taylorsville to the funeral, where my Father's words ran constantly through my head.

"Don't say what you're gonna do. Do it. Make your own luck."

When I returned, I worked day and night, using all the knowledge I'd learned from Frankie Schneider. I pulled out the wires from the instrument panel, throwing every one of them away. I used a piece of aluminum to hold the instruments, rewiring the car with only necessities, and used an old army belt as a seat belt.

That was a major improvement over my first car. Its seat belt was the trace chain off of a horse harness, used to pull a wagon. That piece of chain had been threaded through a fire hose to keep it from rubbing and was fastened by a harness snap. Some drivers tied themselves in with ropes.

I attached a metal part to the throttle for my crippled foot, positioning it right off the fire wall. Then I added an airplane bucket seat and put in roll bars. A lot of guys jumped in and out of cars, but I had to adjust them. It was hard to drive someone else's.

Finally, I finished the black '37 Ford Coach that would be our race car.

That Friday, I returned to West Lanham, where I won the heat, the semi, and the feature in that NASCAR sanctioned race. I was stunned. I'd made that car win the first time I'd raced it, and it's the closest I've felt to ecstasy. Ken Merriott, Lou Johnson, Pee Wee Pobletts, Johnny Roberts, and other veteran drivers were there. No one thought I'd have a chance against those chargers.

Sinclair Oil had representatives at the event, so, unlike many of the races, this one awarded a trophy, which I was presented while being photographed. I'd worked so hard the clothes I wore hadn't been changed in a week.

Saturday, I did the same thing, winning the heat, the semi, and the feature at an outlaw track in Manassas. Since the track wasn't sanctioned, I raced under the name of Johnny Nalon.

Sunday, I went to an outlaw track in Upper Marlboro, Maryland, where I did the same thing, racing as Johnny Nalon against Elmo Langley. A respected local racer, Langley would later work as a pace car driver for NASCAR.

As odd as it might seem, using another person's name was common in racing and there were almost as many excuses for doing it as there were names. Driver Bob Moore retired from racing to become an insurance agent for Allstate under the condition he agree not to drive a race car for the next five years. Knowing temptation would be too much to bear, he stayed away from the tracks. Finally, he decided to go to a race in Dublin, Georgia just to watch.

A friend who was racing told him he was having difficulty with his car and asked him to help. At first, remembering his resolve, he wouldn't do it. Then, he jumped in the car, strapped on the helmet and within minutes identified the problem and fixed it. The car's grateful owner told him to drive it. As unable to resist as an alcoholic, he gave his name as Woody Moore and won the race. To his horror, the win was well-publicized.

The real Woody Moore, who knew nothing of Bob's shenanigans, was repeatedly congratulated for winning the race and blowing the other drivers away. For 25 years, he couldn't figure out what had happened. Then, at the first Georgia Automobile Racing Hall of Fame Association meeting, he met Bob. An honest man, Bob confessed to him what he had done. Woody was greatly relieved to know the whole story, having been baffled for a quarter of a century. Ironically, they live less than 40 miles away from each other.

I continued to race for the rest of the season, winning at Manassas and Marlboro again. With its high banks and wide corners, Manassas was my favorite track, and still is today.

In looking back, our racing was amazing. I was my car's builder, driver, and sometimes, pit crew. Junior Johnson once told me there was no better education than trial and error. He and I learned a lot through that teaching method. We had to in those days.

One lesson I learned, I was lucky to have survived. Bill, Satch and I decided to drive to a Sportsman event in Rochester, New York. Before we began the race, we noticed our gas tank was leaking. I started to drain out the fuel, but was told to leave it in, that the soldering torch wouldn't come in contact with gas.

I was straddling the tank as I soldered when it suddenly went *W-h-o-o-m.* Fire shot out both ends as it exploded, lifting me off the ground. God was watching over us. If that tank had split open, we probably wouldn't be here today, nor would the family jewels.

We'd traveled a long way to Rochester and I was determined to race. Since the tank was destroyed, I ran with my gas can attached to my roll bar.

Except for the end of the season, I usually ran 25 laps. That fall, I went to Bowman Gray Stadium to run a 400-lap team race to gain experience. My partner was Bighead Shause. I qualified outside the pole, and the car was running well, but on the second lap, I hit the guardrail.

The tie-rod was bent and I had to pit and fix it so I could steer. Bighead, thinking I'd come in only for fuel, had disappeared. After losing 30 laps, I made up 16, but my chance for winning had passed.

By the end of the year, I knew my winning wasn't a fluke. Determined to make racing my career, I gave my Mother my trophy and began to look southward.

5

Darlington

First Pass at the Lady in Black

"In the old days, guys just liked playing in the dirt and beating each other. It wasn't about the money. It was about being the best. When I was a child, my neighbor went to Saturday night races. One night my Dad and I went with him. When I climbed up in that grandstand, I found home."

MIKE BELL (Georgia Automobile
Racing Hall of Fame, Historian and Writer)

Although I was driving for Bill Steel, I continued to help B&D owner Brownie. He taught me a lot about aluminum and acetylene welding. It'd be the last job I'd have before racing full time, and by the time I left I'd become a good welder.

Brownie'd been shocked at the races I'd won in my "junkyard car," and working together our relationship grew. One day when we were working, he stopped, looked me in the eye and said, "You wanna drive my car at Darlington?"

I couldn't get "yes" out fast enough; I was so excited to drive that car.

I'll never forget when I first saw the Darlington track. It was the biggest I'd ever seen, and I stared in awe. Its black ribbon of asphalt seemed to wind around its oval course forever. I'd heard rumors about the "Lady in Black." The speedway was alluring and dangerous. Experienced racers bragged about their famous "Darlington Stripes," earned sideswiping the guardrail in turns three and four. Referred to as the "rainbow of courage," the rail brandished its own stripes of paint from the cars. I refused to be intimidated and, after seeing the raceway, changed the toe-in on Brownie's car and adjusted the bite.

Top: #X Rex White and #22 Johnny Cramblitt in a 1954 race at Marlboro Raceway in Maryland. *Bottom:* #X Rex White on the outside of #88 Ed Crouse and #53 Lou Spears at the Marlboro Raceway in Maryland in 1954. (Both are John Ward photographs from the Larry Jendras Jr. Photo Collection.)

Rex White winning at Lanham Speedway in the "Wally Campbell Memorial Race," Lanham Speedway, West Lanham, Maryland, 1954. Bill Webster Photo. (From the Larry Jendras Jr. Photo Collection.)

I was to race in the Modified 100. The Modifieds had racing cams and multiple carburetors. Gas tanks were removed from under the cars and secured in the trunk, to protect them from damage, and fire walls were installed to protect the drivers.

The cars usually had stiff front springs, oversized tires, heavy-duty wheels, reinforced front suspensions, and floating rear ends. The gasoline varied from high test to aviation fuel. Some used methanol alcohol, occasionally mixing in nitromethane. Both concoctions had fumes guaranteed to burn your eyes.

The highlight of the trip was when we checked into a motel in Florence and met Raymond Parks' famous mechanic, Red Vogt. The former moonshiner and driver was known throughout racing circles for his car building, and for suggesting NASCAR's name.

Vogt knew Darlington inside out. He told me the closer I got to the outside guardrail, the faster I'd go. I heeded his advice, dumbfounding Brownie when I qualified outside the pole. Exciting as it was, the experience proved uneventful. The magneto failed and we were soon out of the race. As I hid my disappointment, it was of little consolation to learn of the number of engine breakdowns on the long straightaway. Brownie helped patch one driver's car to get it running. Darlington is the toughest track I ever encountered and that's the reason I considered it the best.

Remodeled to make room for more grandstands, the course is different now. It's turned around with the start-finish line where the backstretch used to be. It's still shaped like an egg, and drivers consider it just as challenging because of its history and its toughness. They talk about those same Darlington stripes. Whereas there used to be a spring and Labor Day race, the Labor Day event has been rescheduled. The track hosts the oldest 500-mile race in NASCAR and attracts more than 100,000 fans.

Shortly after the race, I heard Frankie Schneider had been badly burned in a modified race at Vineland, New Jersey. He'd crashed, and the impact bent the steering wheel against his seat belt, pinning him in. He held his breath, not breathing in fumes, as fire burned his legs. Finally, he was able to wriggle the seat belt loose and get out, but faced a painful period of skin grafting.

He had been using methane alcohol. If he'd been using gasoline, he'd have been dead. In those days, flames were a driver's worst fear and there were no fire suits. I didn't even know what one was. Later, in the Grand National, we put tin foil on the floor on the driver's side with asbestos on top of it. Now, there are special mats and fireproof jumpsuits, shoes, and gloves.

It would be years before I'd have a uniform, made by the wife of a guy named Smitty. Smitty was an itinerant parts supplier who followed the racing circuit. His wife sewed the suit in gold and white colors to match my number four car, then dipped it in boric acid to make it fireproof. It looked good, but I was so used to a shirt and jeans, I rarely wore it.

Not long after Frankie's wreck, Lee Petty captured the 1954 Grand National Championship. It was the first of three, and the beginning of a racing dynasty. Jim Rathman, Herschel McGriff, Herb Thomas, Joe Eubanks, and Buck Baker were also consistent winners. Lee Petty and Herb Thomas were the year's biggest rivals.

Tim Flock temporarily abandoned the Grand National Circuit after his victory was disqualified at the Daytona Beach and Road Course. Plans were in the works for a Daytona super speedway, with completion expected the following year.

Meanwhile, NASCAR became aware of the political clout of fans in a disputed finish at Atlanta's Lakewood Speedway. In a bizarre turn of events, four of the top five finalists were stripped of their placement. Spectators turned into an angry mob, raising such a ruckus all penalties were dropped and drivers placed in the order they'd finished the race. In a later incident, when a driver was fined, the fans promptly took up a collection and paid it.

Jerry Ivey was once driving on a little track in Gray, Georgia, when his left front wheel came off. Since his car stayed upright, he continued to race and won. Track officials attempted to disqualify him, refusing to give him the purse. When irate fans attacked the press box, officials said they'd made a mistake.

Fans at that same track refused to have a race shut down due to track conditions. The owner sent for a road scraper from a neighboring town, then began the first race at 10 P.M., not closing until four in the morning.

In 1954, fans demanded to be heard, and it was also the year of NASCAR's first Grand National Road Race. Billed as the International 100, it was held on the runways of Linden Airport in Linden, New Jersey. Thirteen Jaguars added class and superstition to the race. Al Keller drove one to a first-place finish ahead of Buck Baker, Joe Eubanks, Herb Thomas, and Lee Petty. A Jaguar also came in last.

Despite the excitement, the race was a disaster, with few spectators and not enough money to pay the purse. Later, I would meet Al Keller at Boynton Beach and race with him at West Palm Beach and Hollywood. I didn't win another race that year, but ran some powerful seconds.

In 1955, I decided to race Sportsman in North Carolina the entire season. The guys down there were big-name drivers in NASCAR, and I'd read about their feats in *National Speed Sport News*. Among them was Billy Myers, winner of the Sportsman Championship and the Championship at Bowman Gray Stadium. Satch Steel decided to go along with me and I was glad because he was a great handyman to have around, and I liked to cut up with him.

Passing through Lynchburg, Virginia, we saw a sign advertising stock car racing on Friday nights at Shrader Field. Since it was Friday, we decided to wait so I could race. The competition included well-known drivers Glen Wood, Curtis Turner, and my heroes, Bobby and Billy Myers. I had read about them, and seen them run at the beach, and couldn't believe I would get to race with them.

During practice I followed Billy Myers into a corner where he suddenly braked and I rammed him. I was embarrassed and was sure he'd be mad, but he wasn't. When I apologized, he interrupted, asking how I was able to get my car to corner like that. I invited him to look at my car, and the friendship we struck up that night lasted until he died.

To my surprise, when I went against those hard-charging drivers, I won. Considered "regulars," they were not as happy as I was with my first place.

Al Keller. As winner of the first Grand National Road Race, he drove a Jaguar to first place. (Courtesy Bruce Craig Racing Photo Archives.)

Southern drivers liked to introduce northern drivers to new things, and that new thing was often the wall. Even today I'm called the "Yankee, who took the money and left," by the track promoter. I laugh when I think about it. Maryland is below the Mason-Dixon Line and the only difference between a northern and southern driver is one eats grits.

Satch and I spent the night in my 1946 panel pickup. We slept in it most of the time, unless we went to Taylorsville, where I'd sometimes work on my car in the backyard.

My mother was always happy to see us and Satch was thrilled. The food was a whole lot better than we'd been eating. Health is important to a driver, and I always tried to eat well. When we had money, we ate steak, but we were thankful for potted meat or Vienna sausage.

Our next races were Bowman Gray and Fayetteville, and we went back and forth to Lynchburg, Bowman Gray, and Fayetteville, the rest of the season.

Bowman Gray was a football field, when it wasn't being used as a racetrack. The use of football fields and baseball diamonds was common. We'd circle the goalposts or square off around home plate, go to first, second, and third, and then back home.

There were two tracks around baseball fields in Asheville, North Carolina, and I won on both of them. One was McCormick's Field, and the other, we called "The River." In those days, we raced wherever we could, feeling lucky to be on a real track instead of a pasture.

The third Asheville racetrack was named Asheville-Weaverville, because it was located between those towns. A really nice high-banked half mile, it was my kind of track.

One of the smallest I ran was a one-fifth mile Pennsylvania track, which had a lot of Dutch Amish fans. A racetrack that size is congested, with only 25 cars. It means hub-to-hub bang and knock driving. That track was so narrow two cars could barely go down it, bumping and scraping. The corners were made the same width.

I've bumped a lot of drivers, and they've bumped me. It's like getting up in the morning and putting your clothes on. I like to pass other drivers, but not touch them. You try high and you try low. If you can beat them where they're holding you up, you can get ahead of them. Some guys try to pass in corners. That's where you have less hold on the car. You need to pass coming out of the corners where you have better control. Sometimes it takes a while to size a guy up and get him, but patience was a trait I developed.

Too much success can have consequences, as can running into a guy or blocking the track. Southern driver Charlie Burnette knows this from experience. While he was racing at the Crazy Eight Speedway in Warner Robins, Georgia, in the sixties, another driver rammed him three times. When the third time didn't take him out, the driver rammed the door on Charlie's side, crosswise in a turn.

The car's toe-in was damaged, and Charlie pulled it into the infield. Seeing a volunteer fire truck stationed at the race, he borrowed it, drove it against his tire to make it straight, and got back on the track.

He ran slowly until the other driver passed him, coming off the number two turn. As soon as the driver was ahead of him, he floored it. They went flying down the straightaway, and then Charlie drove him through the wall. This was followed by a fight between the two pit crews.

The next day Charlie was charged with attempted murder and was banned from the track for life. He later learned he'd won so many races that a $1,000 bounty had been offered to take him out.

Within a few days, the charges were dropped, and due to the low attendance after his ban, the track invited him back. He posted a $200 bond and paid the other guy's hospital bill.

In another case, driver Bobby Mitchell was running his 1965 Chevelle street rod, with a 327 and a four speed. He took home a lot of trophies, racing that car. Time passed and one day when he went out to work on it, the car was gone. The police found it hidden in woods in another county. The engine and transmission had been taken and the rest of it burned. Later, they traced the engine to another race car where it was still performing well.

There's always high tension during a race, and you can't let it get the best of you. On super speedways, a bad move will bite you and it's a good way to do yourself in. Stay focused, and always treat others fairly, because tomorrow it may be reversed. If you see two guys knocking each other, hang back. Sooner or later they'll wreck and you'll get past them.

You can politely rub, but don't spin. Don't take the guy out of the race. If you knock a guy out, you haven't won. It's supposed to be racing, not beating and banging each other out of the way. When you're a lap down, you should yield to the guy in the lead. That said, I know bounties are still offered today, particularly at short-tracks, on guys who consistently win.

I avoided touching others as much as possible since every scrape and dent just meant more work, and I was relieved Billy Myers had taken my accident well. Billy, a big guy with short-cropped jet black hair, loved to race. A hardworking driver, he ran well on dirt and asphalt. That season, we raced together all summer long. We helped each other, and he let Satch and me use his garage. Satch, being so young, was the brunt of a lot of jokes. Good-natured, he endured as much as a kid could stand related to girls. Billy's brother Bobby liked to cut up as much as we did, and the four of us had a good time and a whole lot of fun.

Rex White in a 1936 Ford Coach, taken in 1953 or '54. "You can politely rub, but don't spin. If you knock a guy out, you haven't won. It's supposed to be racing, not beating and banging each other out of the way." (Photograph courtesy Motorsports Images and Archives.)

Racing was a twenty-four hour a day job, and we ran three to eight races a week. Our humor helped keep us going when the schedule was tight, and as soon as a race was over, boom, we were out of there.

"With sponsorship, I could build a competitive car today. I can rub my hands over car parts and know what they are in the dark, and if I could choose my car, it would be Chevrolet." (Photograph courtesy Motorsports Images and Archives.)

There were many times when I was up all night, taking naps beneath the car on the creeper. We worked on every piece of the car, including the frame.

That was one of the reasons racing back then was so challenging. When we won, we did it ourselves and we felt proud. It was meaningful to beat the other drivers and the racetrack, but we also wrestled exhaustion and lack of sleep. That's one reason tempers were hot and races were often fought on adrenaline highs.

When I raced, most drivers were responsible for everything on their car and there were few exceptions, but Sammy Mallock was one of them. He didn't know how to change a tire, but he was a good driver, winning in Delaware, New York, and New Jersey.

Since funds were low, most of us were always improvising. Whoever said "Necessity is the mother of invention," must have been a race driver. At times we used parts over and over. The way we had to experiment was running a race. If we failed, we'd have to go back and start all over again.

There are so many improvements today. If we'd had radios everybody could have communicated better, and having a rear end cooler would have won me more races. You can buy it now, already made up to put in your car.

The engines today are ready to race. They've been tested on a Dynamometer and there's no guesswork to it. Everything's perfect. It's all handmade. All you have to do is stick it in. Each one has 15 to 20 minutes of Dyno time on it, at different RPMs. But, as exciting as it may seem, it's just not the same. We put our engine in the car ourselves in our shop, then we revved it up and if it sounded all right, we went to the track.

With sponsorship, I could build a competitive car today. The cars and chassis haven't changed much except aerodynamically, and in order to be a winner, you have to have knowledge of that. If you had all the pieces of a car in a pile and told me to put it together and win a race, I could do it. I'd have to study it, but it would be easy. I can rub my hands over car parts, and know what they are in the dark, and if I could choose my car, it would be Chevrolet.

6

The Early Years
Running with the "Hot Dogs"

"In the 1960s, the Mason-Dixon line was the dividing line between stock cars and Indy cars. We didn't have Darlington. We didn't have Wilkesboro. Racing up north was nothing like racing in the south."

TOM FRENCH (Transplanted Northerner,
Director of Operations, ThunderRoad, USA)

In the fifties, we had to have physical strength. I was strong from my days on the farm, and as a mechanic, but race cars were hard to handle without power steering. I was out of racing when that came on board, and we had a heck of a time running on dirt.

I caught my share of teasing because of my size. Sometimes drivers offered me a high chair, and fans said all they could see was my helmet, but there were some advantages. I was so small I could crawl beneath the instrument panel, and my lightness kept from adding much weight to the car. Since I didn't have the strength of a Cale Yarborough or Tiny Lund, I made the chassis work for me, as much as I could.

Some drivers resorted to gloves, but I needed the feel of the car. You can tell more about a car when you're steering bare-handed.

Today's cars have quick steering ratios and power steering. You don't wear blisters on your hands, and all the NASCAR drivers have to wear gloves. Taylorsville driver Harry Gant was one of the last to race without them. A carpenter, at 39, he was the oldest driver to win a Winston Cup race, and became one of NASCAR's Top Fifty Drivers.

67

I learned to put rubber around my steering wheel and cover it with black tape, to give better grip and control of the car. My hands were often covered in calluses, blistered, and bleeding. A hundred-mile dirt track could wear the skin off. Once when we were at a carnival in Taylorsville, I went to a fortune teller who tried to guess people's work from their hands. He couldn't guess mine and I won the prize.

Despite what some believe, racing is a sport and drivers are athletes, but it's not just because of physical strength. A person has to have talent, concentration, good reflexes, and quick decision-making skills. The mental part is a heck of a lot bigger than most people realize. If someone spins out in front of you, you've got to know what to do fast.

For instance, at Daytona, if a car spins in a corner, it gains momentum and rises toward the guardrail. It's going to spin down and inside and you've got to notice that. When it comes down, you can go by it on the outside. If it hits the rail, the momentum and centrifugal force will still bring it down. You've got to be able to time it right, and know how to handle it differently on the straightaway. Many of us were uneducated, but we understood engineering and physics.

In the old days, there were fences at a lot of the races and not much contact with fans. I liked the fans and liked to be accessible. You couldn't sit down in a restaurant without people wanting to talk, but it was hard to get to us at the track.

People learned you could talk to the drivers if you brought a beer. When my fans gave me a cold one, I was thankful. I'd traded Cheerwine for Coke or that beer, but never got into hard drinking. I was just glad when I had something to eat and replacement tires.

I won three Sportsman races in 1955, two at Lynchburg, the other at Fayetteville. Winning attracted advertisers, who'd pay to put signs on your car. When they'd ask, "Can we take out an ad?" my answer was "Yes!"

Superstition was a big thing in racing, especially with southerners. We couldn't have peanuts in the pits, have numbers that read the same upside down, or wear anything green. No one wanted to use the number thirteen.

Peanut fear went back to midget and sprint car days when Ted Horn flipped and was killed. Peanut shells were found in his car and his pit. Once, a driver saw peanuts, refused to race, packed up his gear and fled.

Fireball Roberts became superstitious of the "Kiss of Death," having wrecked three times after kisses from beauty queens. His fear of the racetrack beauties was finally overcome by Mary Ann Mobley. Miss America of 1959, she broke the jinx by placing a surprise kiss on his cheek before he won the Daytona 500.

Ivan Stephens' race car, with a real black cat on its hood by his helmet and trophy. "Ivan raced in a green car, with a black cat and the number 13 painted on its side. He'd eat peanuts and throw the hulls on the track, horrifying the other drivers." (The Ivan Stephens Photo Collection.)

Ned Jarrett's car was number 11. He used to take every number 11 route to a race he could find. He'd go out of his way to locate it and traveled on it as much as he could, always running well when he did.

Gif Egan, an Irishman, put a four leaf clover on his door to bring him luck, but Fred Lorenzen claimed he had no superstitions. He admitted he put stock in feelings, which were good when a special fan showed up at his race.

Of course, there were rebels then, as there are today. Ivan Stephens had a green car, with a black cat, and the number thirteen on its side. He'd eat peanuts and throw the hulls on the track, horrifying the other drivers.

In racing you always want to go to a track planning to win. Without that attitude, you'll be a loser. Sometimes, racers say "I had bad luck," but you make your luck, like my Father said. You surround yourself with good people with talent. If you've got a lot of horsepower, you work on the chassis. If you've got a good chassis, and not enough engine you work on horsepower. You check your springs and shocks, and make sure your gear ratio's right. Problems that cost me races on small tracks were usually related to gear ratios and rear axles.

Frankie Schneider used to say that it wasn't horsepower that got you around the track, it was the car. It may look like luck, but it's all in the preparation, and little details make the big things work.

Another thing you have to do is focus. The morning of the race or qualifying, I always liked to get away from the bull crap and sort my thoughts. No two racetracks are the same. Each has a different surface, banking, turns, entrance, and exit. Climate affects them, too, as well as geography.

We were always at the track early and I learned how to look at it, and know, how to set up my car. I could tell by sight whether to run higher or lower, but I could feel how the car ran best, and that was usually the fastest way.

Bobby Allison once said I reminded him of a checkers player, always looking ahead. He claimed I'd be looking at turn two, before I was out of turn one, and knew where the slow cars were. In those days, you had to be a smart driver to get your next meal. Dumb drivers didn't last because they couldn't afford it. But then, there weren't many dumb drivers, anyhow.

In early racing, drivers were thought to be either bootleggers, thrill seekers, speed demons, or a combination of all of them. The public thought most of us didn't have enough sense not to risk our lives.

Ned Jarrett's father used to take him to races when he was a child. When Ned said he wanted to race, his father sat him down and told him not to do it, in no uncertain terms. He said racers had bad images, and no respect. Mr. Jarrett had worked hard to build a good image and wanted to keep it. He didn't want his son associating with bootleggers.

Ned spent his career proving there were very good people in racing, and it didn't matter who you associated with, you could earn respect. He not only lived up to his father's ideals, but became a role model motorsports spokesperson. His son Dale is now a driver and keeping up Ned's good image.

There are good and bad people in everything, and to me, bootleggers weren't bad. Some were prominent in my community, and they had to make a living like all of us. Making a living at what I was doing was a challenge. Our biggest obstacle was generating money to survive, trying to make ends meet and paying all our bills. I became an expert in working on my chassis, being able to judge when it needed a change, knowing what to do to make it race faster. Nothing made me happier than solving problems, learning how to do something differently, or figuring out something new, then winning a race. I found setting a car for one turn could slow you down in another turn and I had to be able to adjust the car to handle both.

You can't buy experience. Somebody's got to show it to you, or you've got to live it. I've seen a lot of race cars go by on the track and I learned how to observe what was going on. I'd plan my fuel economy before the race, guessing how to stretch it. I'd want to run as lean as I could, but not burn a piston. The leaner you run the more horsepower you'll develop. A powerful car makes a powerful driver, and I'm the first to admit I liked power.

To qualify, you use all the racetrack, trying to get around the fastest way. You go around corners and learn how to approach them.

The time of day affects a track's temperature and how it runs. In the old days, if you were given a two-hour morning period to qualify, you'd go out there quickly. Those who waited would qualify late. Eventually, nobody would go out, waiting for the track to cool off and change. Later NASCAR solved that by making people draw for position to qualify before the race.

In racing, when you've got ten people working on the car, it's a group job. When the car works well, you've all done your homework, but when you climb in the race car and strap on the helmet, it's up to you. You prove yourself again and again. Statistics in racing are just the surface. The important things take place behind the scenes.

Once the flag drops, there's plenty to do and nothing should cross your mind but winning the race. You think about strategy and how to dodge cars, figure out how to pass, and avoid making mistakes. You've got to remember your tires, oil pressure, and temperature, and watch all your gauges. I had to predict when my car needed water. Tire wear and track conditions affect a car's handling. Incorrect tire pressure can cause a wreck, and it affects how you go through corners. I equipped my car with trap doors in the right front floor and in the right rear and opened them with cables. They allowed me to look at the tires and tell if the tread was low, while I was running. Tire pressure on a race car is everything.

Spinning is one thing you want to avoid. Spinouts flatten your tires. You'll have to change them on a super speedway, because the car will vibrate so badly you'll have to stop. If your oil pressure drops, you can make repairs. If you're not alert, you'll blow your engine. If there's money in your pocket, you're not in trouble, but, if you're broke, that's all she wrote.

During races, I always studied the moves of my competitors. I wanted to know how far I could push them and to be familiar with their strategies. This

71

was especially important when I was drafting. Some I could trust for consistency; others were unpredictable. Staying on top of what's going on means everything. All drivers know about the big things but the little things, like wedge, are what put you ahead.

I had good eyesight and depth perception when I was young, and my mind was constantly going. I'd assess every possible situation and be prepared for the worst. When I was approaching another car at high speed, I was able to judge my stopping distance. Aware of everything around me, I could even spot wrenches on the racetrack. I've found screwdrivers, box wrenches, pliers, and ratchets. When I saw them during practice, I slowed, reached out and grabbed them for my toolbox.

On the other hand, like everybody else, I sometimes made stupid mistakes, too many of them to count. The maddest I've been, and the most disgusted, has sometimes been at myself, like when I've tried to get past other drivers too early.

Interestingly, you can take two cars and set them up the same. Put two different guys in those cars, and one guy will go faster. The same is true with cars. The same driver will drive two cars, seemingly alike, and one will go faster.

Satch and I worked hard in preparing our car. At only 15, he was eager to learn and soon became my sidekick. Remembering Frankie Schneider and my father, I was tough, not letting him quit until he got the job done. Satch stayed with me all summer, working as a one-man pit crew, my truck serving as our home. He always managed to stay on his "see food" diet. Anytime he saw food, he had to eat.

When he went back to school, I slept in Billy's garage. Sprawled on an old beat-up sofa, I covered my body with blankets to keep off the rats. They were big, and late at night, I felt them scampering over me.

Racing southern style, flat out and belly to the ground, I ran hard and wide open, doing everything on my own. Edith had a job at an egg candling plant in Washington, where they'd hold eggs over a light to be sure they were good. She stayed in an apartment in Tacoma Park with a roommate named Ruby. We rarely saw each other, as it was a struggle to make ends meet, keep up my car, and increase its speed.

Meanwhile, the whole field of racing was having troubles of its own. AAA, NASCAR's main competitor, tried to compete with its own strictly stocks division, and wrecks attracted widespread attention.

In March, driver Larry Crockett was killed at a crash at Langhorne Speedway. In May, Mike Nazaruk burned to death on the same track.

Two-time Indianapolis winner Bill Vukovich was killed as his car spun out of control, landing upside down, a flaming inferno. Other deaths included Jerry Hoyt, Manuel Ayulo, and Jack McGrath.

European racing fared even worse. During the 39th running of the LeMans, an inexperienced driver hit another car, skidded, ricocheted into a crowd of spectators, and exploded. The carnage was unbelievable. With deaths totaling 100, the news made headlines around the world. The public responded with such an outcry that American politicians, again, tried to get the sport banned.

As before, Bill France restored reason and calm. He pointed out how racing innovations had benefited passenger cars, making them safer, and the strides NASCAR had made. He said NASCAR was expanding and would soon add more supervision to all kinds of tracks.

Automakers backed him. They'd already realized how racing boosted marketing, as cars winning on Sunday meant Monday sales. People loved to see the car model they drove winning a race. Ford and Chevrolet joined Hudson, putting dollars behind NASCAR teams. Their sponsorships would take racing to another level, as did their advertising campaigns. Strangely, Chrysler did nothing, yet company products managed to win 27 events.

When Herb Thomas moved from a Hudson to a Chevy to win the 1955 Darlington 500, Chevrolet fans went wild. Thomas, sometimes called the "Unknown Hero of Stock Car Racing," was one of the best early drivers. Like me, when he first saw racing, he decided to become involved in it. He started out as a car owner, then became a driver and jumped into the NASCAR Grand National circuit during its first season. Famous for not backing off, he eventually won over 20% of his starts in Grand National racing, having teamed up with car owner and driver Marshall Teague and mechanic Smokey Yunick, during his beginning years.

Meanwhile, another car owner entered the scene and made a big impact. Karl Kiekhaefer, owner of Mercury Outboard, formed his own racing team. A prosperous businessman, he dressed his pit crews in uniforms and hauled his cars inside trucks. This added professionalism and class.

Kiekhaefer set the stage for major automakers' high-visibility involvement, backing drivers such as the Flocks, Speedy Thompson, and Norm Nelson. Tim Flock took 19 poles that year in a Kiekhaefer Chrysler, establishing a NASCAR record, and winning the Grand National Championship.

My stay with Billy Myers was coming to an end. Since my car was beat up and ragged, and he could outrun me, he suggested I build a new one, which I did. He and his brother Bobby helped me paint it and when we finished it really looked good. Competitors again, Billy and I decided to run separate races, so we both could win. He went to Fayetteville and I went to Lynchburg. Both of us won.

7

On-Track and Off-Track Shenanigans
Racing's Just Part of the Show

*"I attended my first Grand National race in Asheville-Weaverville when I
was a nine-year-old kid. As I sat in the splintery old wooden grandstand, the
first car I saw was a pretty gold Chevy, with a big red number 4 on its doors.
That car led from start to finish, and was driven by Rex White."*

GREG FIELDEN (Author of *Real Racers*)

In October, I headed to Florida to run the South Florida Circuit. I lived
in the attic of race fan Pete Jones, who had a garage and compassion for drivers.
My friend "the car thief" lived there, too, without a race car. The guys down
there were hard to beat, but I won two or three races that year.

Brownie's son, Bill, was working in a gas station nearby. When one of his
customers wanted someone to drive his car to Rochester, I jumped at the chance
to be home with Edith for Christmas.

The car's owner flew, leaving me his Cadillac convertible and girlfriend.
We headed north, stopping to see Bobby Myers in Winston-Salem, where I
tried to show off my "new ride and honey bun," but knowing me well, he didn't
fall for my story.

Despite driving through a terrible snowstorm, we reached New York, safe
and sound. The owner paid me $160.00 and I caught a Greyhound bus to
Maryland, where I did a lot of explaining about the girl and the car.

Moving Edith out of her apartment, I took her with me to Boynton Beach,

Florida, in our '51 Mercury. We were so broke; I borrowed $20 from Bill France, Jr. as we passed through Daytona.

I stopped by Fish Carburetor and was talking with their driver Fireball Roberts, when he said he was going to West Palm and blow me away. That didn't happen, as I outran him, but we both lost the race.

Edith and I rented a room in a private home that had a side entrance, and Pete Jones let me set up my "garage" under a tree in his yard. Shade tree mechanics choose their trees for their good sturdy branches, needed to hoist their engines in and out of their cars. All of my work was outside, but the tree was strong and the climate was good.

During a race in Hialeah, I broke a crankshaft and spun in my oil. Bobby Johns hit me, followed by several other cars. The seat broke and I fell over. Edith was watching from our truck, but never got out. By this time, she accepted my spins and crashes.

I alternated between Hialeah, Hollywood, and West Palm, winning five races, and a bunch of seconds. All of my wins were at West Palm.

Early in 1956, Alvin Hawkins, the promoter for Bowman Gray Stadium, called. He asked if I would drive in the Daytona Grand National for Max Welborn, whose father owned Pioneer Chevrolet. I was thrilled and agreed.

The car, an assembly line model from General Motors, was right off the showroom floor. I was glad to have something new, but it wasn't adapted. They put in a roll bar and a seat belt, took the hubcaps off, and considered it ready.

That same weekend I drove for my old friend Brownie in the Modified race in his car. Before the race I noticed a skip in the engine at high speed. He told me to drive down the A1A backstretch wide open, and he'd listen.

I drove by him at over 100mph. Concentrating on Brownie, I missed the warnings for the south turn. As I rounded the beach a car was stopped on the course, with a couple taking a bathroom break for personal business. I barely missed them and slid on by, as the terrified woman attempted to pull up her pants.

The incident taught me a powerful lesson. I learned I could go deep in corners, and control my car. Daytona qualifying was always on the beach in a straight line on the "Flying Mile." No one was able to practice on the backstretch, because it was a highway. We were only allowed to go fast on it during a race and I wasn't supposed to be on it going that speed.

We were able to fix the skip, but the transmission broke in the race and I couldn't finish. No one else completed the entire race. It was called ten laps short, when a Northeast wind sent the tide up onto the track.

I raced on Sunday in the new car, but since it wasn't set up, I placed near the end.

Edith was sick every morning, and went to a doctor who confirmed she was pregnant. A proud father-to-be, I helped pack our things and moved her to her mother's in Maryland, so she wouldn't have to deal with my schedule. It had taken a dramatic toll on our marriage. When I wasn't out of town, I was in the garage. I saw a lot of drivers wreck their marriages, sometimes when they'd gotten too frustrated. Often a car and a marriage would blow up at about the same time.

I moved in with the Welborns in Yadkinville, North Carolina, where I worked on their car to make it competitive. Their clean sheets and towels were a step up from the Myers' garage. They had a large home and a maid, and served southern-style meals. Satch would have loved to have been there.

I raced all year in the Welborns' Chevrolet, just running Grand Nationals, and ran second in the Short Track Division. I got a lot of poles by adapting my car to the race-tracks. Every time I went to a new one, I qualified well. Nearly all of them were dirt at that time, but all tracks vary. One time they're slicker. One time they're hotter. Each race is different. I approached every one as a problem to be solved, first finding its groove.

The car will pick a track's groove, if you let it. That's the position where the car runs fastest. Most of the time it's the lowest point, but that's not always true. After a race you can usually see it, because it's turned darker.

Dirt tracks present the biggest challenge, because all of them have different character and you need to be innovative in order to win. For instance, on dirt, you can make your own groove. Ned Jarrett did that once and won a race.

One night in Valdosta, Georgia, he was not running well. Everyone else was on the bottom of the track, so he decided to go higher. He began working on making a groove, lap by lap, an inch at a time. He held onto that groove, making it wider, and going faster, very carefully and very precisely, even when lapped. Finally, he worked it up to 18 to 24 inches and blew the other drivers away.

The biggest problem on dirt was visibility, particularly at night. Most of the tracks had poor lighting and it was hard to read your instruments. Sometimes rocks would beat holes in my gas tank and shove the windshield into my lap. We learned to protect the gas tank with a sheet of plywood, held by a steel band.

I always ran with a shaker screen over the radiator, but when races ended, fans, and drivers, were covered in grime. I had to make pit stops just to clean the windshield. Some drivers ran without one, which resulted in injuries from flying debris.

During the Grand National in Tulsa, the dust got too thick to see. Frustrated, Lee Petty stopped and jumped out of his car, then ran from the pits to the flag-stand. Seizing the red flag, he stopped the race. Ticket money was refunded and the event was never completed.

I learned a lot about running on dirt after rain. I found if I'd get at the end of the pack, the front cars would knock the mud off the top of the track, clogging their radiators while mine would stay clean. Soon, I could pass them. I won two races that way.

Racing wasn't glamorous back then. There wasn't anything to be glamorous about. A lot of fans got in with money earned picking up Coke bottles, and they were much more loud and rowdy than they are today. Some fans got so drunk they didn't know who won the race until the next morning when they read the newspaper. I'd have liked to have had the money they spent just for beer. Concession stands stopped serving drinks in bottles when they were thrown through race car windshields.

Butch Nixon tells of sitting behind a couple with a cooler, who were three sheets to the wind. When the cars came out, the woman claimed she couldn't see over the people in front of her. The man, too drunk to think, told her to step right up on their cooler, and she did. Styrofoam, ice, beer, and the woman, flew in every direction.

Another time, Butch and his father-in-law were sitting in the stands talking when a guy came up and held a knife at the throat of the man sitting next to them. As Butch was nudging his father-in-law and telling him he thought it was time for them to leave, the guy with the knife burst into a grin. He greeted the fan and asked how he was doing, then said he just thought he'd come up and scare him.

The worst fight Butch remembers occurred between two women. They were fighting over which driver was best and got to fussin' and cussin', finally thrashing it out on the ground in a travel home's septic tank waste.

Not everything was down and dirty. Good things happened, too, even romance. In 1955, driver Tommie Clinard met his wife at the track in West Palm Beach, Florida. He and his business partner, John Fort, had built a new car. John was going to race it that night, and then they were going to take it to Hollywood. But, instead of winning, John rolled the car three times down the front straightaway, and tore it up.

Pretty Marilyn Berry was covering the race for a magazine. After the wreck, she caught Tommie's eye when she walked over to look at the car and interview John.

Marilyn's father was Bud Berry, a NASCAR Pit Steward and Starter. Her mother, Florene, ran a souvenir stand. At the end of the race Tommie and John were waiting to get paid when they saw her typing her story in the souvenir stand. Tommie told John, then and there, he was going to marry that girl. A week later, Tommie took her to the track in Hollywood and within two years they were married.

They've been together 46 years, and Tommie says they've had three children, ten grandchildren, and several race cars. When you think of it, race cars are like children. They need a lot of attention or they'll cause aggravation, and when they perform well, you're proud of them.

North Wilkesboro was one of the first tracks on which NASCAR competed, and the site of some of the highest interest in racing. One year, a fight broke out in the grandstand. It started because one fan liked one car and one liked another, and turned into a hate-filled brawl. The argument grew until several hundred fans were involved. That fight was so big I could see it from the track. When they started throwing things at the drivers, the race was stopped.

Today, racing's more about drivers. In those days, it was all about cars. Fans would pull for a driver they didn't like if he drove the right car.

Before every race, someone would ask, "How many of ya'll are for Ford? How many for Chevrolet?" Ford and Chevrolet fans were always ya-yaing each other, with Pontiac supporters jumping in. Then some would pull for the Pettys and their Plymouths. Their arguments often turned into drunken free-for-alls.

I know about fans because I once was one. I picked Frankie Schneider as my favorite driver because he was the best, and because of the color of his maroon and white number 88 car. Color was a big deal, as was make, because you could pick your favorite car out of the pack. I've known fans who wore Chevrolet shoes and Chevrolet underwear.

Of course, I was partial to Chevrolets, but also liked Porsches. A Porsche is one of the best cars for handling. Its center of gravity is close to the ground, and it's designed to corner. You don't drive that car, you wear it like a suit.

My brother Heindl was as loyal to driving Ford as I was to Chevrolet, but his pastor was definitely a Chevrolet fan. At Heindl's funeral, the preacher got in the last word about their rivalry. He said he'd decided he might drive a Ford to prevent getting a ticket.

Today, types of cars don't make much difference to me as long as I'm riding, and all cars look good when they're in the winner's circle.

In the old days, other things besides cars would set fans off, and it could be fun to watch. We'd be waiting for the race and someone would yell, "Look at that!" We sat in the pits when we weren't busy and looked at the scenes in the infield. Some were dens of iniquity, a "Never-Never Land" with motor homes turned into brothels.

There was an awful lot of drinking, and liquor makes you do funny things.

"Racing is the only sport in which the industrial world crosses the business line and enters sports. Racing has something for everyone, the big guy and the little guy." Rex White (right) shown with Georgia Governor Sonny Purdue at an Atlanta Motor Speedway event in 2003. (Courtesy Anne Jones Photo Collection.)

Law enforcement provided a lot of our entertainment, breaking up quarrels and maintaining a semblance of peace, but the fans enjoyed foolhardiness.

While I was working on this book, I attended several races at Atlanta Motor Speedway. During pre-race activities, I sometimes hitched a ride in a police car. In March of 2003, Joel Cope and I caught a ride with a Henry County police officer. As we rode by a group of fans, they stared at us as we passed. One looked at the officer and yelled, "Get 'em." Another hollered back, "Yeah, they done something stupid!"

Another time, a bunch of people watched a guy too drunk to drive get into his car. To their relief they saw him climb into the backseat. Thinking he'd decided to sleep it off, they were startled to hear his voice bellow out, "Who stole my steering wheel?"

Once, we were in the infield in Atlanta, when two girls got naked and started a mud fight. Two or three more joined them, and everyone came out of the pits. I tell you that drew a crowd. In the South, there's a difference between "nekked" and "naked." When you're "nekked," everyone knows you're up to no good.

Although they weren't usually nude, fans weren't nearly as dressed up then as some are today. They often had more off than they had on. A pair of shorts and no shoes or shirt wasn't uncommon for guys. If it was hot, most clothes got pulled off anyway. Things always got rowdier as the day wore on, especially during long periods of waiting. If there's anywhere you can be yourself, it's at a racetrack.

Seating was tight, and with people so jammed up against each other, it wasn't unusual to be hit with a beer can, or peed on. Accidents were always happening in the stands.

At the short track at Roanoke, there was an argument between fans and pit crews, and they got up on my truck to fight. When they began swinging blows, I crawled beneath it.

Sometimes it was the fans, and sometimes the drivers. A losing driver tried to stop Eddie Mac-Donald from winning by filling his engine with syrup. When Eddie went to race, the heat turned that syrup into candy.

In a 1956 race in Fayetteville, Bobby Myers and Curtis Turner got into it while racing their 1937 Ford coupes. It ended with Curtis forcing Bobby into the wall.

At the end of the race, Bobby was so mad at Curtis he picked up a tire iron and ran to confront him. Curtis picked up a thirty-eight pistol, held it where Bobby could see it and asked Bobby where he was going with the tire tool. Bobby quickly told him he was just looking for a place to put it down.

One of the funniest things to happen occurred at Martinsville. The famous mechanic Slick Owens pretended he was me while on a date. The next day when I came in first,

Curtis Turner. "In a 1956 race, Bobby Myers and Curtis Turner got into it while racing their 1937 Ford Coupes. It ended with Curtis forcing Bobby into the wall." (Courtesy Bruce Craig Racing Photo Archives.)

"The famous mechanic Slick Owens once pretended he was me while on a date," shown here (at left) with me at an autograph session in 2002. (Courtesy Anne Jones Photo Collection.)

the girl heard the announcement and ran up to Slick, saying, "Rex White, Rex White, you won the race." That wasn't the only time Slick did that. Another time at Daytona he called himself "Cotton" Owens.

No one was safe from drivers' pranks. Once, Linda Vaughn, who was Miss Firebird, found her sports car propped on its end against the wall of the hotel in which she was staying.

When a driver scandalized his neighbors by painting "nekked" women on his car, they called the law. Within a few days those women were clothed.

Richard Abercrombie had a '34 Ford with a picture of Woody Woodpecker on the side. Today, his car is still remembered as the "Flying Pecker."

Old-time drivers could be wild, especially homegrown ones raised around dirt tracks. They often worked behind old barns, or in garages, struggling to see with single light bulbs, relying on flashlights to help them. When mamas and wives had enough, drivers hid their cars at a friend's house, or parked them at local gas stations.

Racing is the only sport in which the industrial world crosses the business line and enters sports. That's why it attracts so many blue-collar supporters. Racing has something for everyone, the little guy and the big guy, the mechanic and the business executive. Everyone plays a part, even the preacher. In the old days if you raced, preachers talked badly about you. Now they cut short their sermons to get to the track in time for the feature.

I attended a Raceway Ministries service in Atlanta where Brother Eddie Barton said we were going to go to heaven and God was going to ask us if we'd cheated. God was going to know if we'd cheated. He said he thought sometimes when drivers put on a helmet, it constricted their brains. Warning us sternly against sinning, he said if we didn't watch out, we were going down the track wide open, headed for Hell.

8

Fanfare and Friendships
A 300-Pound Kid Named Tiny Lund

"My favorite driver was and still is Rex White, and my favorite car was his gold #4 Chevrolet. It had a revving, roaring sound I could recognize. I remember it to this day, and call it Gold Thunder."

LARRY HINSON (NASCAR Fan)

Fans are everything. They are the most important part of racing, more important than drivers and cars. Without the fans, there wouldn't be any racing, but sometimes they're treated like dirt. They deserve a lot more consideration than they're given because the people in the grandstands are what it's about.

After I became a driver, fans supported me, boosting my morale. I found there were people who followed me from grandstand to grandstand, just like I did Frankie. I got a kick out of seeing them. There was a group of Dutch guys from Pennsylvania whom I could count on to be at each race. Even today, I get letters from countries around the world and it makes me feel good. I've received letters from England, Germany, France, Australia and Canada and I've begun to save the envelopes to keep a record.

One of the most meaningful descriptions I've been given came from a fan. He said I wasn't an underdog, I was a role model, and that made me proud. It's something I always work to be, because I want everyone to know they can be a champion, and people often influence others when they're not aware of it.

One fan says he taped my number four to his go-cart when he was a child.

"Sometimes fans become friends." Rex White (right) with fan and friend Larry Hinson at an event at Thunder Road in Dawsonville, Georgia, in 2002. (Courtesy Anne Jones Photo Collection.)

When another fan, University of Kentucky Professor Allan Hall, was a toddler he taped a number four on his red pedal tractor. Pretending to be me, he would make as many laps as possible on his porch on weekend afternoons.

Allan remembers, as a teenager, listening to the radio for racing news and reading *Motor Trend* and *Hot Rod Magazine* in his school library. He says my being a winner, despite my size, had an impact on him. He felt if I could be successful, he could be too. Many fans have said that, and I am glad my being a "runt" has been a good thing.

Sometimes fans become friends. Harlow Reynolds and Larry Hinson are examples. They were racing fanatics in the fifties and sixties and are special to me today. We like to talk about the old days, and they have given me "Rex White" memorabilia I wouldn't have otherwise. Another fan, John McKenzie, tells how he used to put together model cars like the ones I drove. Since there were no decals back then, the lettering was all handmade.

One weekend I was going to race at Council Bluff, Iowa, and had a mechanic put a 131 transmission in my '56 Chevrolet. When he did, he didn't put in any grease. It wouldn't have made any difference as I was going to tow

"Wayne Hale and Harlow Reynolds are two fans who have become friends. They have given me 'Rex White' memorabilia, I would not have otherwise had." (Courtesy Anne Jones Photo Collection.)

it on the ground without the drive shaft, but when I got to the track, I put the driveshaft in, went out to warm up, and tore out second gear. Not having a spare transmission, I took the one out of my '56 Chevrolet tow truck and put it in. Since it was the wrong ratio for that track, I didn't run well, and afterwards, I had to change the transmission back.

Two guys came by, one named Kenny Miler, and a giant of a man called Tiny Lund who was 6' 5" and nearly 300 pounds. They helped me change the transmission, and Tiny invited me to his house to eat and shower. A driver, he was temporarily out of racing due to lack of funds. He'd been in a race where he'd flipped four or five times going down the straightaway, tearing up his car.

Tiny was good, especially on dirt, because he was raised in a cornfield village. He loved getting sideways, laughing as he threw dust all over the spectators. When he was able to get his finances together, he came east, bringing Kenny with him. Neither one of them lived in Iowa again. They stayed at Billy Myers' shop and I used to help Tiny set up his car. He never did get a steady sponsor, but when he drove, he did a good job and when he was able to rent a house in Taylorsville, his wife joined him.

A great outdoorsman, Tiny liked to hunt pheasants and fish. He held a record for the largest bass caught in Santee Cooper Lake. It weighed over 50 pounds.

The difference between fishing and racing was in racing you couldn't lie. You might fib a little, but the records would show it. That's not to say drivers don't tell tales.

Of course, if you're as old as Georgia driver Charlie Bagwell, you could almost make up your racing career. Most people who first saw him race are no longer living. At 76, he still takes his "U2" car to the Senoia, Georgia, race-track, and has raced over 50 years, but those who know him say he's really slowed down. They say he has to race at a track with lights, because if he enters a day race, it'll be night when he finishes.

Tiny and I spent a lot of time on the Catawba, because he loved the rivers like I did. We did a lot of jug fishing. We'd tie a line to a milk jug and let it float. Pretty soon, a big 'ol catfish would get on it and that jug would go flying across the water with the fish trying to get away from the hook. We'd put a bunch of jugs out at night, and then hunt for them in the boat with a flashlight.

I also had a trout line and would tie a rope across the water, tie lines to it, then go back, take the fish off the hooks, and re-bait them to catch more. That's the lazy man's way to fish, but my Dad thought even that took too much time. He made fish baskets out of wood. He'd lace pieces of wood together to make the basket, make a funnel in it with a door on the side, bait it with meal, tie it to a tree and drop it into the water. When a fish went in to get the meal, he couldn't get back out. After my father finished his chores, he'd pull the basket up, open the little door and we'd have supper. I tell you, my Dad loved catfish and he could skin them quicker than you can say "Boo." He had a special post he skinned them on. A lot of those fishing techniques aren't legal now, but they were a lot of fun back then.

Tiny later opened a fish camp at Moncks Corner, South Carolina, where he kept dogs, cats, chickens, ducks, and a monkey. Funny and likeable, he was always playing tricks and his pranks were not only constant, they were obnoxious. He liked to fight, but seeing his size, nobody wanted to risk being hit. Tiny looked like, and reminded me of, a 300 pound kid. Race cars were bigger in the old days. If they hadn't been, he wouldn't have been able to get into one.

Chicago driver Tom Pistone and I were the smallest Grand National drivers. Tom was even smaller than I am. Tiny used to pick us up, throw us over his shoulder like sacks of flour, and carry us around.

"If you're as old as Charlie Bagwell, you could almost make up your racing career."
Charlie Bagwell racing his "U2" car at the Senoia Speedway in Senoia, Georgia.
(Courtesy Anne Jones Photo Collection.)

The Charlotte track had a cheetah they kept in a cage. Cheetahs are rough, but Tiny would take the thing and wrestle it. They'd get down on the ground and roll and play.

Tiny was always trying to aggravate us. In the garage, he was like a bull in a china shop and just about drove us crazy. When he was in there, we couldn't get any work done. He upset everything and I believe he could have broken an anvil.

Once, we went to Darlington about a week ahead of the race. He started throwing water off the roof of our hotel, then, began throwing people in the pool. My pitman Slick Owens threw in the janitor, then a policeman, gun and all. Jim Rathman was there and laughs about it today.

Motels were sites for lots of race-driver shenanigans. One night, after an evening of drinking, Joe Weatherly drove his car into the pool.

Tiny and I remained friends, until he died in a wreck at Talladega. He was such a good driver; he was voted one of NASCAR's Top Fifty, and was popular and loved by his fans.

Toward the end of the season, I raced at Flat Rock Speedway in Detroit. I sat on the pole, ran well, and thought I'd win the race. Before I could finish, I ran over a hub and tire, tearing up the car. It upset my pit crew, but I took it in stride, and, boom, we were out of there. Despite the wreck, my performance attracted the eyes of Chevrolet. They gave me so many parts, I had to get a cattle truck from Yadkinville and go back to pick them up.

I was close to finishing second in Short Track points, so to keep my spot I went to California to run two races. Satch was in school, and I took a kid called "Johnson" from Yadkinville, to be my pitman.

Donald Johnson was a young boy who worked in the Chevrolet dealership, and had never been out of Yadkin County. His parents were reluctant to let him go, since he was only 15, but somehow he convinced them it was okay. He was as excited as anyone I've seen and saucer-eyed all the way, taking in the sights of the West and tasting tacos for the first time.

Nothing like Yadkinville, North Carolina, California was a leader in the streets. Something would happen on the West Coast and make its way east. The state was known throughout the world for its hot rods.

I ran second in the first race at Gardena and was leading the second race at San Jose when the hot wire came off the starter. The engine quit, but with Johnson's help, I was able to fix it and finish. Gardena was famous in the early fifties for televising jalopy and midget races. San Jose was a high banked one-third mile track with a really weird groove.

I ran into Johnson recently. He still lives in Carolina, but his mind's full of memories of the trip we made. It meant a lot to a kid from a place as small as Yadkinville.

We left San Jose on a Monday for a race in Greensboro, North Carolina. It took almost a week of cross-country driving day and night. There were not any interstates back then, and only the big towns had four-lane highways. It took four or five days to get out to California from the East Coast and another four or five to get back. I finally let Johnson drive when we reached Alabama, and we arrived at the race on Thursday.

The Greensboro track was a half-mile dirt at a fairgrounds. Ralph Moody and I tangled on the track and my car ended up on its side. Johnson helped me get it right side up and I continued running. That was the last race of the season, and the last time I drove for Max Welborn.

Kiekhaefer was still on the scene in '56, backing his drivers with high-dollar cars. He supervised his men with military strictness, but paid them top salaries. One of the first black drivers worked for him and was named Charlie Scott.

Kiekhaefer was the first to bring scientific principles into racing, the first to emphasize excellence and education, and the first to make racing professional.

Prior to his entry into NASCAR, there wasn't even an electric wrench. He brought electric wrenches and bottled oxygen. Pulling his cars in straight trucks, he'd not only bring spare parts, he'd bring extra engines. If our engine blew, we packed and went home.

It was a first-class operation for him, and for others a wake-up call. He caught the eye of Ford and, indirectly, Holman-Moody. Kiekhaefer dominated so many races, fans and officials grew tired of him and complained. He was gone by the end of the season, but left a legacy never duplicated, setting a pace that changed racing forever.

The biggest trend in NASCAR that year was the emergence of factory teams, intensifying the rivalries between cars and fans. Ford, Chevrolet, Plymouth, Pontiac, and Dodge were all hiring drivers.

NASCAR was expanding, sanctioning more tracks, and the purses were increasing too. Buck Baker took the Championship in a Kiekhaefer Chrysler, with winnings over $34,000.

I won one race in '56, ranked 11th in Grand National Final Point Standings, and came in second in Short Track Division. The highlight of the year was August 26th, when my daughter Brenda Mae was born. Her birth made me prouder than racing, as I loved my family, and she would become my biggest fan.

My greatest accomplishment was being invited to Detroit. I bought a new Robert Hall suit to meet with Ed Cole, who was the President of Chevrolet. It was the first suit I owned and I thought it was nice, until I saw those of the Chevrolet executives. It was then I learned what a $400 suit looked like.

Three-time Indianapolis winner Mauri Rose was there, having become the head of the Performance Division. Rose, with his ever-present pipe and mustache, was known for his arrogance, but had the statistics to back it up. Despite my inexpensive attire, Mauri recommended, and I was given, Chevrolet sponsorship.

9

Hot Dogs to Hamburgers, in a Hurry

At Last, Chevrolet Sponsorship

"The first race I saw on T.V. was the old Daytona Firecracker 250 on Wide World of Sports. Of course, it was in black and white, and the announcer stood in the grassy area between the track and pit road."

ALLAN W. HALL, C.P.M. (Executive in Residence, Kentucky State University, Racing Enthusiast)

I jumped from hot dogs to hamburgers in a hurry. My new salary was $650 per month, more money than I'd ever made in my life, and I had an expense account.

The first thing Chevrolet did was send team members to East Point, Georgia, outside of Atlanta to set up our headquarters. We got our tools and equipment together and set up a Central Avenue garage. Ford's racing team used the name Holman-Moody. We were Southern Engineering.

Holman-Moody was already making history. Originally Peter DePaolo Engineering, it was first headed by DePaolo, who was the 1925 winner of the Indianapolis 500, and was a high-budget operation. Their drivers included Joe Weatherly, Curtis Turner, Jim Reed, Ralph Moody, Bill Amick, and Marvin Panch.

The other major automakers also had teams. Ray Nichels, formerly on an Indianapolis crew, headed the Pontiac team through his shops in Highland, Indiana. Cotton Owens and Banjo Matthews were two of his drivers. Everett

"Cotton" Owens grew up around his father's garage and cars were his life. Beginning his career as a racing mechanic, he was soon driving, and his ability seemed natural. He placed second in his first race, at Hendersonville, and stayed at the wheel for the next 12 years.

Ohio-born Edwin K. "Banjo" Matthews was known for his modified wins and for having the thickest eyeglasses. How anybody could see on the track with such bad eyes was beyond me. He eventually improved his eyesight through surgery, but although his driving was good, he never won a Grand National.

Bill Stroppe, of California, managed the Lincoln and Mercury teams. North Carolina driver Jim Paschal and Modified Champion Billy Myers drove for him. Mechanic Guy Wilson worked with the East Coast drivers. Oldsmobile had a two-driver team with hard chargers Lee Petty and Ralph Earnhardt. Plymouth, a Chrysler division, was managed by Ronnie Householder, a cigar-smoking former midget car champion and engine genius. Ankrum "Spook" Crawford was chief owner and mechanic. The soft-spoken and modest Johnny Allen was the driver for the one-car team.

Our team consisted of seven members, Bob Welborn, Alfred "Speedy" Thompson, Buck Baker, Possum Jones, Jack Smith, Johnny Beauchamp, and me. They added Frankie Schneider on my recommendation and we were ready to conquer the speedways.

Bob Welborn was a two-time convertible champion who'd placed fourth in Final Point Standings in '55. He liked fancy cars, changing them faster than his underwear. I've seen him trade twice in one day. Once he had a Cadillac convertible for a short time, and then traded it for a push-button DeSoto. The next day, he came back with a Chevrolet. He always had money in his pocket, and the rest of us borrowed money from him when we ran short. Always cutting up and never serious, he drank Wild Turkey every day when he wasn't racing and you always saw him with a Tampa Nugget cigar. We could read his mental outlook by that cigar. He held it in his fingers when he was doing hard thinking and if it was ragged and chewed, we knew things were bad.

Speedy and Buck were ex–Kiekhaefer drivers. Speedy was a tough North Carolina country boy who raced with the roughest. I'd been in a lot of races with him. Elzie Wylie "Buck" Baker was one of the most enduring drivers in NASCAR history. I was only nine when he began his racing career. He'd won the 1953 Darlington Southern 500 and was still going strong.

Possum Jones was the hardest person to get out of bed I've ever seen. We couldn't get him up to go to work with us. Finally, I got the bright idea of buying cherry bombs and putting them under his bed. The house stunk, but they got the job done.

Possum had been driving for Bob, came along with him, and got more than a salary out of the deal. A single guy, he went to a nearby store to buy some clothes and fell in love with the woman who waited on him. It wasn't long before they married.

Jack was a local Atlanta charger, who won 21 Winston Cup races by the end of his career. He was a master strategist, known for his sharp tongue, and was often seen clocking competitors with a stopwatch. He was also the first driver to use a two-way radio and to fireproof his racing uniform with boric acid.

Johnny Beauchamp was a friend of Tiny Lund and like Tiny, was born and raised in an Iowa cornfield. He came from the IMCA Circuit, where he drove for Dale Swanson, and Dale came to Atlanta with him to fix up his car for Daytona.

We looked at each other and liked what we saw, a tough gang of drivers ready to roll. Frankie and I were to cover the short tracks; Bob Welborn, convertible; and the others would handle the speedways. Hired only weeks before Christmas, we had seven cars to build for Daytona, and there was no time to spare.

We rented a nice brick home on Cofield Avenue in an upstanding neighborhood in Hapeville, near Hartsfield International Airport. There were seven of us in that house, sleeping all over the place, three and four to a room, and driving our neighbors insane. Nobody could get any rest. We'd go in and out all hours of the night, spin our wheels and slide to a stop. Girlfriends would come and go. I never knew what to expect and there was always a party.

Despite the chaos, we were anxious to begin driving, but not prepared for what lay ahead. Our supervisor was more concerned with saving dollars than winning. Despite company backing, he forced us to spend hours and hours in junkyards, searching for parts. When we couldn't find what we needed, we had to "make do." Although we were a Chevrolet team, we had to use old Ford drive shafts to make our sway bars.

Soon, we were angry and frustrated and our hopes were dashed. It was well into December before we got started, and we weren't building cars until the first of the year. The season was only a month away and the team was in chaos. Our chances for success were growing slim and patience was wearing thin. I quickly began fabricating cars, putting in roll bars, sway bars, and shock mounts. The only tools we had came from my toolbox.

How could we compete against Bill Stroppe or Holman-Moody?

Our experience at the Daytona Beach and Road Course was disastrous. We were disorganized and exasperated, in the process of hiring more people and behind on everything. We had not had time to prepare and the other

95

company teams were ready. Johnny Beauchamp managed to come in second despite mechanical failures. Buck Baker placed fourth, Speedy Thompson eighth, and I came in ninth. Frankie Schneider went to the front before his shifting linkage bailed and he had to struggle to finish. We'd worked hard to make a good show, and did better than expected for the shape we were in.

Finally, Chevrolet became aware of what was happening to the team and fired our supervisor, replacing him with Indianapolis driver Jim Rathman. A California native, he was a prematurely balding, blond, small-framed man who began his career with drag racing. He moved to the Midwest after high school and gained experience driving anything he could, including sprints, stock cars, and midgets. He was known to avoid dirt tracks, preferring instead to race on the more stable asphalt. A key to his success was his approach to racing as a business. Like me, he relied on consistency rather than daring. Despite his many wins, he'd rather place second or third than risk not finishing, and his no-nonsense style was just what we needed.

Rathman took over immediately, helping us organize our shop and get on track. Experienced and knowledgeable, he added expertise that was a shot in the arm that increased our spirits.

I was double-dipping, working as a driver and a mechanic, plus collecting my winnings. It had been a matter of necessity without personnel, but Jim put a stop to that, refusing to let me build cars, and assigning me two mechanics. Neither had much racing experience, but they were good at following directions. They performed well when I took the time to tell them what to do.

After Daytona, we started over, building new cars. Edith was still in Silver Spring, Maryland, so I went home. No longer allowed to do the work myself, I told the mechanics how to build my car over the phone.

Frankie Schneider was shocked and said I couldn't know what I was doing, but when the car was delivered he changed his mind. I warmed it up, adjusted the air pressure and wedge, and then let him drive it. He liked it so much, he had his car set up the same way. Jim gave him two crackerjack mechanics to help him, Louie and Crawford Clements.

Still improvising, I installed padded backrests in the cars for shoulder support, and was the first to use jackscrews. They raise and lower the car to change its weight from one wheel to the other. Keeping the right wheel higher helped in the corners, and made the car handle better.

One week when our pay was late we gathered a truckload of ginger ale bottles, traded them for their deposit money at a local grocery and bought food. I was buying the ingredients for our usual low-budget supper, which was a huge pot of Spanish rice. When I got home, there was a letter on the door from

"I was double-dipping, working as a driver and mechanic plus collecting my winnings." (Courtesy Motorsports Images and Archives and International Motorsports Hall of Fame, Talladega, Alabama.)

a group of our neighbors. When I opened it and read it, I was shocked. We were accused of operating a house of ill repute.

I didn't know what that meant, but it sounded bad. I went over to our shop and told Jim Rathman the neighbors were accusing us of running a house of ill repute and I didn't know what that was. He called me a dummy and informed me it was a whorehouse.

There I was, 26 years old, and I had never heard it called by that name. The neighbors had been trying to get us evicted, and I understood why. They'd made a lot of comments about us and as young and wild as we were, I can't blame them. There was something wild going on every night.

The house was up on a hill and some of the guys would go get drunk at a drive-in restaurant called Chicken Haven, known for its good-looking waitresses. They'd come back and run up the bank all the way to the steps and park. When it was muddy, we'd slide back down and spin around in the yard. We were a mess.

We had trouble keeping the house clean and that drove me crazy. The sink stayed full of dishes, and dirty clothes were strewn all over. There was only one bathroom and that was a popular place. As soon as I could, I brought Edith and Brenda down and we moved into the Alamo Plaza, an extended-stay motel inside Atlanta. The best part was that we could walk across the street and eat at the Catfish King. I gave Satch my old family Mercury, bought a new Chevrolet for Edith, and thought I'd made it to heaven.

Our 1957 Chevrolets looked good, and a nicely restored one brings in a chunk of change today. The most popular was painted black and white, had a fuel injection engine and was called the "Black Widow."

My life seemed too good to be true, and it was. We raced the fuel injection engines only once before NASCAR outlawed them and then we were back to four-barrel carburetors.

West Coast Short Track Division points went toward the National Short Track Division Championship, so Chevrolet decided to send Frankie and me to California to race. We supervised the building of our cars in Los Angeles.

We spent a lot of time flying back and forth, but when the cars were completed, our first West Coast race at Gardena was canceled by rain.

We flew back to run in a short track race at Bowman Gray Stadium, then flew back to California, where we were able to run the rescheduled race at Gardena. We flew back to the East Coast so we could run a race in Evansville, Indiana, then back to California to race at Balboa Stadium. That race was rained out, and we went back to the East Coast again. More time was spent in the air than on the tracks. We'd built great cars but left them out there after racing them only once.

Chevrolet had top-secret proving grounds that I'd heard about, but never seen. Closely guarded, the place was rumored to be the site of mysterious testing and engine experimentation. It was part of the research and development division, and no cameras or unauthorized visitors were allowed. You had to have security clearance to enter. The place was so secretive, even GM's different divisions were assigned special areas. Like the military, Chevrolet had chosen the desert for clandestine activities. Located outside of Mesa, Arizona, its thousands of acres were surrounded by an impenetrable circular fence.

Since I was no longer working in the garage, I was invited out to run tests on tires.

Firestone had been dominant in racing, but Goodyear came onto the scene in '56 and by 1957, they were highly involved. Tire improvement was gaining importance now that more tracks were paved, and cars were traveling at increasingly high speeds. The two companies were now competitors, and like winning cars, winning tires increased customer sales.

Because of its mild, dry climate and flatlands, Arizona is rich in racing history. I arrived to find the weather unusually warm. I stayed about a week, testing tires, and accidentally murdering jackrabbits, who came onto the track at night. Then I rejoined our team to race.

By the end of June, Chevrolet won six Grand Nationals under our factory banner, three of them short track, won by Frankie and me. Most importantly, I beat Frankie in Manassas, showing him I was not only a driver, but one to be feared.

Our success was short-lived. That summer, under public pressure, Chevrolet and the other factory sponsorships pulled out of racing. When Ford publicly backed out, employees John Holman, a former trucker, and race driver Ralph Moody took out a bank loan and bought the operation. At Chevrolet, there were no takers. Each driver was given our car and a tow truck, to race on our own.

I'd helped my friend Hall Moose get a job with our team as mechanic and when Chevrolet cut us loose, we stayed together. Moose was a country boy from Taylorsville like me. He'd later have a car repair shop there, which he still has today.

We went back to Maryland, where Edith and Brenda were living with Edith's mother. On fire to start racing again with good equipment, I renewed my friendship with Bill and Satch Steel. Moose and Satch, who was then 17, became my pit crew.

One day, Moose and I were riding from Baltimore to Washington to store parts, when we were hit head-on by a drunk driver. The truck was knocked over, Moose's face was cut up, and my ribs were torn from my side. Barely able to move and unable to race, I loaned Frankie my car and crew.

He ran four Grand Nationals, winning three, and placing second in the fourth. I paid him a driver's salary, and used the rest for the crew and myself.

When the season ended, I rented a shop for my race car, letting Eddie Skinner park his in our garage. Eddie was a character if I ever saw one. In those days, drivers sometimes put castor oil in their engines for lubrication. One night, he put his cloth racing helmet on, heated castor oil in a pot on the stove, took a deep breath of the smell, and pretended he was at Indianapolis.

The first time I met Eddie was at the old Charlotte three-quarter mile speedway. I was just returning from Darlington, where I'd run Brownie's car and was pulling it with a tow bar back to Maryland when I stopped at Charlotte to see the Grand National race.

I was standing in the pits when Eddie came flying by, put his brakes on real hard, and saw me standing by the concession stand. He unbuckled his seat belt, then pulled a quarter out of his pocket and handed it to me to buy him a Coke. I bought the Coke and handed it to him. He drank it straight down, poured the ice and what little was left all over him, re-buckled his seat belt, and took off into the race. He'd stopped for a drink!

Eddie Skinner wasn't serious about anything. I was at the Hollywood Speedway in Florida and a lot of drivers were standing by the fence looking out on the racetrack. I remember Bob Welborn, Jim Reed, Jimmy Luellen, a bunch of us. Eddie walked up, looked at the racetrack and announced as if in amazement, "This racetrack has turns in it." Everybody looked at him like he was crazy. He said a lot of dumb things like that for effect.

Eddie left home one night for a loaf of bread and didn't go back for 15 years, having spent the time in Nevada. When he returned to Maryland, his children were grown. He told people he found his wife in bed with another man, but that was okay: He knew they couldn't do anything because they weren't married.

A health food fanatic, Eddie wouldn't eat anything grown on top of the ground, saying it was contaminated by nuclear fallout. He often ate rutabagas for breakfast, and he built an underground fallout shelter.

Believing dirt was less dangerous than soap, he rinsed his dishes in plain water, refusing to use detergent. His theories must have agreed with him. At age 77, he was still winning late model events.

By fall, I was racing and Moose and Satch were back with me.

In Toronto, I was leading the race and was almost to the finish line when Jim Reed spun me. He sped on and took the win. The fans were so irate they wanted to fight. They broke his windshield and tried to turn over his car. Terrified, Reed ran to the tower, grabbed the microphone, and told them the victory was mine. He meant it, and gave me the purse.

Jim was tough at any flat one-quarter mile racetrack. We raced together again in New York, at a football stadium in downtown Buffalo. Not giving him a chance to come close, I charged hard and won. I also defeated him when I placed first in Fayetteville. I liked that one-third mile track with its high banking.

Despite Chevrolet's pullout, 1957 was a very good year.

10

Staying Focused
Drivers Need a One-Track Mind

"We used the same car. We'd bolt the top on for a hardtop race or take it off for the convertible race. If hardtops and convertibles ran together, they gave separate prize money.
"You got extra money if you came in first in the convertibles. We ran convertible in a lot of races because we didn't have to win to make big dollars."
JOHNNY "PETE" PADGETT
(Mechanic for Joe Lee Johnson)

A fan once said he'd never seen me show emotion after a race. It isn't that I don't have feelings; it's that acting on those feelings can bring problems. Anger can make things worse and rejoicing can come too soon. As a driver, you've got to keep yourself in the right mental state, because there are so many things to distract you. It's important to keep your mind straight, and not get emotional. I'm not easily offended, and what people say doesn't bother me. I've been talked about by professionals.

I don't let things depress me. The only thing that can depress you is something you don't have control over, and most problems solve themselves in 24 hours.

There's a lot of pressure around a track. You can get your dander fluffed in a hurry. I try not to dwell on problems, just crush them and put them past me. But, I do admit to hardheadedness, trying to do things my way.

Now, I can get mad, but the older I've become, the more I've mellowed, the more I've seen hotheadedness just doesn't work. With age I've learned to rationalize things. Most of the time when people get mad, they're mainly mad at themselves. I've learned if I get angry, to just walk away, because frustration can cause bad decisions.

Fatigue can cause bad decisions too. When you're tired and have a problem, you stay with it. It's better to give it up, and sleep on it. The next morning you'll have it figured out. You're better off if you just remain calm, no matter how bad things are. You've got to be tough enough to face whatever occurs.

Throughout my racing, and even now, when hard times come, I think of my father, who never wallowed in what could have been. If a crop failed, he planted another one. If a field produced well, he made it produce well again. He held his focus.

I held my focus using the lessons I learned from him, and from those fields.

Ned Jarrett says, "Race drivers need a one-track mind." His play on words is true. You have to maintain concentration, no matter what happens. If you hang in there, are consistent, and plan what you're going to do, you'll get the job done. If you fail, that's behind you. You've turned that page over. Now, look ahead.

As a child, I was trying to escape, not only the farm, but my father's words. As an adult, I learned to meet problems head-on, no matter how cruel life seemed.

The year of 1957 was a rough year for NASCAR, with the exit of the factory teams. Others withdrew after an accident injured spectators at Martinsville, including an eight-year-old boy.

Martinsville's short half-mile length has always been challenging. Its 800-foot straight-aways abruptly halt in its hairpin curves. Drivers push to their limit, then are forced to reduce speed with their brakes. When Billy Myers and Tom Pistone tangled, Myers's car sailed over the wall.

The industry was also under fire from the Automobile Manufacturers of America Association for high horsepower advertising and building performance cars for the street. Safety activist Ralph Nader became involved and they were afraid if they didn't pull out, the government would come in.

Veteran drivers were also concerned about safety, related to the numbers of inexperienced drivers crowding the circuits. Bobby Myers was killed, and Fonty Flock hurt, after amateurs forced Flock into a spin. His injuries were so serious, he never raced again.

As before, Bill France pointed out the industry's gains, citing safety features resulting from competition. He persuaded racetrack promoters to up their prize money, and helped racing teams with travel funds. Former Chevrolet team driver Buck Baker claimed his second Grand National Championship, placing in the top ten in 38 out of 40 starts.

Dave White had raced in a lot of motorcycle races, and in '58 he wanted to drive Grand National, and asked me to build him a car. He was managing a truck stop, and the owner backed him. I agreed, as a way to pick up extra bucks, and got Louie Clements, the mechanic from the Chevrolet race team, to come and help me.

Louie and I finished Dave's car and helped him get started. The first time he raced, the rear suspension broke, so we redesigned it, made it stronger, and then it ran fine. By this time, Frankie Schneider, Dave White and I were all running cars. I won the first race of the year in Fayetteville, getting a little over $600.00. Lee Petty came in second and Tiny Lund third.

In the past, tire manufacturers had given tires to drivers, but the practice had been recently stopped. Frankie and I ran tire tests for Goodyear at Trenton, New Jersey, in preparation for a 500 miler.

The tire wear was excessive. The surface condition of the track was rough, and it wore those tires out in a hurry. We were still counting pennies and the purse was small. If we raced, the tire bill alone would be outrageous.

The promoter of the race was Pat Purcell, Vice President of NASCAR. Frankie lived only 15 miles from the track, and was a good drawing card, so Purcell promised each of us free tires if we raced.

Frankie registered first, and sat on the pole, but was given no tires. Frustrated and angry, he turned around and headed home, passing me on the way and warning me. I went home, too, never signing in.

Purcell, angered by Frankie's appearance, then withdrawal, banned him from NASCAR. That was hard on me, as Frankie was my friend, my favorite driver, and my closest competitor. There were lots of people I liked to beat, but it's fun outrunning someone you know. That excited me more than beating someone I didn't know.

In spite of the ban, Frankie continued to race at outlaw tracks, which were tracks not sanctioned by NASCAR. He ran Modified at Flemington and Vineland, New Jersey, and Nazareth, Pennsylvania.

Georgia Short Track driver Buck Simmons is known for winning a thousand races. Frankie won that many, or more. I bet he's taken a checkered flag more than any driver alive. He won so many trophies he had to keep them in his shop and there was grease running out of them.

During midsummer, another great driver emerged, who would become the winningest driver in NASCAR history. Twenty-one-year-old Richard Petty entered the July 19th event in Toronto. He came into the sport with a "bang," crashing his car halfway through the race.

In August, a new track was opening in Nashville. The promoter called me offering appearance money, wanting to be sure he had enough cars and

J.B. Day, shown above, in 2003. "As a child, J.B. Day reached Lakewood Speedway by bike. Consumed by a love for racing, he'd leave Easley, South Carolina, and pedal for days, sleeping in the woods at night." (Courtesy the Eddie Samples Photo Collection.)

well-known drivers. I accepted and Moose went with me to serve as my pit crew.

The racetrack had an odd groove, which I found right away, and there was a bar outside the track, with the best draft beer in the world. The track was also popular with drivers because of its good hot dogs. You always remember the bars, and good places to eat. Daytona was famous for its frog legs, California for Mexican food, and Boston for prime rib and lobster. Near Atlanta, we ate at Thomas's family restaurant in the Farmer's Market, and Bristol, Tennessee, had a steakhouse that was unreal.

I sat on the pole and was leading the Nashville race, when a right front wheel broke and I hit the wall. I wasn't hurt, but the car was heavily damaged. The impact bent the frame and tore loose the A-frame. The race was won by convertibles, which placed in the first four spots.

Later, whenever I raced at Nashville, I always sat on the pole, always able to find that same winning groove.

After the race, I took my wrecked car to Cotton Owens's garage in Spartanburg, where Louie Clements was working, but there was so much damage that I headed back to Silver Spring.

The car was in such bad shape, I never rebuilt it, running Dave White's in the Southern 500, and two other races. The last Grand National of the '58 circuit was held at Lakewood Speedway in Atlanta and, without a ride, I drove as Joe Eubanks's relief driver in a Pontiac.

In the '30s, '40s, and '50s, Lakewood was one of racing's most popular tracks. It was also one of the most dangerous. A one-mile flat dirt oval, it surrounded a scenic lake, its quiet setting the opposite of its reputation. At least a dozen drivers died there during its heyday and it was known throughout the Southeast.

As a child, J.B. Day reached Lakewood by bike. Consumed by a love for racing at an early age, he'd leave Easley, South Carolina, and pedal for days, sleeping in the woods at night. He'd get there late Saturday and camp in the water-truck by the lake, where he'd fight off mosquitoes. The hardest part was getting his bike over the eight-foot fence. He was thrilled when he found a drainpipe under the third turn and could ride right in. It was only a one-way ordeal, as he could always find a way to bum a ride home.

Day later became one of the region's most famous car owners, and is renowned for his annual "Raymond Parks's Birthday" parties which hundreds of people attend today.

Local people usually rode to Lakewood by streetcar. To avoid the ticket fee, they would go to the hill across the road at South Bend Pool. If the wind was blowing right, they got covered in Georgia red clay. It seeped into their pores and bled out in sweat like diluted blood.

The track was poorly maintained, with dust often blinding drivers and leading to wrecks. They'd try to follow the car in front of them, but sometimes couldn't even see that. Once it got so dusty, Wilbur Rakestraw and Bob Flock turned up missing and the announcer had to get the flagman's attention to stop the race. When the race was red-flagged, they were finally found trying to get out of the nearby retention pond.

In one race, Ed Samples was badly injured when his car went out of control and turned over eight times coming down the straightaway. Because he believed roll bars and welded doors were for sissies, his doors were held shut by leather straps. Every time the car flipped, the crowd saw him hanging out of it.

The most horrible accident of all occurred in 1950 when Skimp Hersey's car crashed and flipped, and then burst into flames. Covered in gasoline, he leapt from the wreck on fire. As fans watched, the burning man collapsed on

J.B. Day, shown above, seated in the ruins of the old Lakewood Speedway grandstands in Atlanta, Georgia. (Courtesy the Eddie Samples Photo Collection.)

the ground. The next day he died. His death was accompanied by photos in Atlanta newspapers. The public was so shocked, they called for an end to the sport.

When Atlanta Motor Speedway was built, Lakewood never ran another Grand National race, although visitors can still walk through the site today. There are many such tracks in America, haunted by memories of screeching tires, and screaming spectators.

The most unusual closing of a raceway is told by Jimmy Mosteller, a veteran race announcer called "Voice of the Speedway." The founder of the Hav-A-Tampa series, and well known in the South, he's announced more events than anyone in racing history. He was in the announcer's booth at Middle Georgia Raceway in Byron, when a stranger came in. He told Jimmy to announce the track was going to close. Since Jimmy didn't know him, and didn't think the owner'd sold out, he decided to wait.

After the race, the man came up again and showed Jimmy his badge. He asked questions about moonshine and whether or not Jimmy had seen an illegal

An aerial view of the remains of Lakewood Speedway, Atlanta, Georgia. (Courtesy the Eddie Samples Photo Collection.)

still. Jimmy said no, that he'd come to do his job, then head back to Atlanta. The man kept asking questions about where the still was. When Jimmy continued to say he didn't know, the man led him to the ticket booth. He opened a trapdoor and motioned for Jimmy to follow him. He led him to a still, located beneath the third and fourth turns."

Mosteller was and still is, tough. According to *Pioneer Pages* writer Mike Bell, when Bill Cooley opened a dirt track in Athens, Georgia, in the mid-sixties, he asked Jimmy Mosteller and other track veterans to help him. When they arrived, the track had been wet down, but was still too dusty to race. An amateur heat was lined up and ready, but seeing the track's condition, Jimmy motioned for more water on it. Seeing Jimmy's signal as the cars came out of turn four, the flagman quickly changed to the red flag instead of green. The drivers stopped with the exception of one, who sped to the front and hit Jimmy.

As former driver Charlie Padgett remembers it, the guy ran right into him, knocked him in the air and then ran over him. Jimmy rolled underneath that car like a rubber ball. If it had not been an amateur car, it might have sat low and killed him.

Jimmy Mosteller in front of his collection of racing memorabilia. Called the "Voice of the Speedway," he founded the "Hav-A-Tampa" racing series and has announced more races than anyone in racing history. (Courtesy the Eddie Samples Photo Collection.)

Charlie, the first one to him as he lay on the track, says Jimmy looked up, saw him and said, "That tore up my cigar. Have you got a cigar on you?"

Jimmy, known for his trademark cigar, loved the early days of the drag strip, but he soon found he was a heck of a sight better announcer than a racer. He is now in his eighties and still calling races today. As a 50 year participant, his memory's as unbelievable as his experiences. He says, "It all started on dirt, and by golly, between the racing and the fighting, I enjoyed it." He has announced at over 40 tracks and claims when he started announcing, he got the best seat in the house.

Beloved for making everyone feel part of the show, he's also known for his gift of gab and is never far away from a microphone. When he threatened to write his memoir, a friend laughed and said he'd better start cuttin' trees; because he was gonna need some paper.

Speaking of Jimmy's signaling to wet down dirt tracks brings back memories. Dust was held back with large quantities of water, salt, calcium, oil, or anything else handy that worked. Whatever was used we wore, since it blew all over our skin and clothes. I remember the dryness of my lips from the salt and the calcium.

At the end of the '58 season, I sold my car to Jimmy Parsley and Bill Schneider so I could get money to build another one for '59. They fixed it and raced on outlaw tracks for years.

During '58, NASCAR was changing, with dirt tracks being paved and cars' speed increasing. More drivers and spectators were attracted to racing events. It was a non-exclusive sport open to everyone.

Unlike football, all you did was qualify, not try out for a team. Race cars gave their drivers a similar feeling of power, and notoriety. Those such as Fireball Roberts gained celebrity status. He won six out of ten starts, placing eleventh in Grand National Points Standing. In a bizarre turn of events, he claimed $32,218.00 in purse money, compared with Grand National Points Champion Lee Petty's $26,565.00. He did it by entering only big money races at super speedways. I finished seventh, easing ahead of well-known driver Junior Johnson.

Roberts was the first to receive the Florida Sports Writers' Professional Athlete of the Year Award. The honor boosted the perception of drivers as professional athletes.

The year was a sad one for me, as my friend Billy Myers died. He had a heart attack during a Sportsman race at Winston-Salem's Bowman Gray Stadium. Haunted by his earlier accident, in which spectators were injured, he managed to slow the car, steering it safely off the track.

11

Daytona and Drafting
Beginning of the Super Speedway Boom

"Without a doubt, Rex was as determined as you could possibly be. If he decided to do something, he'd do it. He'd work on his car, then, drive it. He knew everything there was to know about a car, and 'most everybody copied what he did to his chassis."

CHARLES "SLICK" OWENS (Mechanic for
Rex White and Holman Moody)

At the end of 1958, I was still working with "Moose" and Satch. Chevrolet secretly gave me a ride, but since it was a passenger car, I used only the frame and body.

Satch decided if he was old enough to patch up a race car, he was old enough to drink. He grew a beard so he wouldn't be carded if he ordered a beer. With the beard and the weight from his see-food diet, he looked adult.

Still as excited about racing as ever, he worked himself ragged, staying around me so much, he seemed like a son.

While I was building my new car, I raced the Champion Speedway at Fayetteville in Dave White's number 40. When mine was finished, my old number, 44, was taken, so I applied for number four. NASCAR agreed. I was pleased because it had been Billy Myers's Sportsman number. That suited Louie Clements because we were friends, and he'd used "4" racing Modified. We were getting ready for the tri-oval asphalt at Daytona and Louie, hard up for money, had come to help us.

The Daytona International Speedway was a long-time goal of Bill France.

111

It was the biggest built since Indianapolis, constructed at the turn of the century. They were the largest oval tracks in the world, until Talladega, and today Daytona symbolizes NASCAR.

Daytona was also the highest banked track, and marked the beginning of the super speedway boom. Its tri-oval allowed for more grandstands, and brought drivers closer to crowds, but its biggest plus was high speed, leading to drafting.

I discovered drafting in the track's first Grand National, behind boxy '59 T-Birds, and there were lots of them. I could come up behind, take my foot off the throttle, and, amazingly, coast. When I pulled out, I hit a wall of air, and if one got behind me, it was like pulling a sled.

When I was following a car and got close, as soon as I dropped into its draft, I could catch it, picking up three or four miles per hour. I had to pull back or I'd run right into it. Even slow cars could keep up if they tailed a faster one. If a guy came up behind you you'd both go faster, and the more cars in line, the higher the speed. We went around faster than ever.

Drafting soon became a science. Rumor has it Dale Earnhardt, Sr. could see a wall of air, and manipulate it. True or not, "The Intimidator" used it to his advantage.

Anytime you're traveling over 50 miles an hour, wind affects you. Mariah is a mighty force. A car going through wind at 100 miles an hour can rise off the ground. Every mile per hour faster you go, the more wind affects your control of the automobile. I'm no genius or scientist, but I understand it.

Another thing we discovered was the slingshot pass. We found if we got in back of another driver's draft, we could wait until the time was right, jump out and shoot past him. We did it on the last lap; otherwise, he'd ride your tail then do the same thing.

At Daytona, a car, on the other side of the track, will change your speed. It's different now because of the new aerodynamics. If you jump out from behind, today, you almost stop.

Once, we went to the track with a winning car, but the head gasket blew and Tiny Lund won. To tell you how fast we were going, I could run behind Tiny, jump out, break the draft, and roar right on by.

During the '59 race, we were averaging about 135 to 140 miles per hour. I was running pretty good when the shaft froze in the distributor. It pulled all the wires off of the plugs. I got back in the race, too behind to win, placing 26th out of 59 cars.

Lee Petty and Johnny Beauchamp finished the race in almost identical time. At first, Beauchamp was thought to be the winner. After days of furious protests, photo analysis proved Lee Petty won. Johnny Beauchamp had been in the winner's circle, kissing the girls, but he had to mail those kisses back with that announcement.

Marshall Teague was tragically killed in a test race, run for a future race at Daytona, less than two weeks before I ran. He was driving the "Sumar Special," a new Indianapolis car built by Chapman Root. He'd lapped up to 174 miles per hour, and was hoping to break the 177 miles per hour track record set by European Tony Bettenhausen. The car flipped wildly end over end, traveling over 1,500 feet, and sending him 60 feet into the air. He came to rest, still in his seat, over 100 feet ahead of the car.

Bill France had announced a United States Auto Club (USAC) Indy Car race for April and had set up practice sessions. It was during one of these that Marshall Teague died. Later, when the race was held, Jim Rathman won, but George Amick lost control of his car while coming in third. It careened into the retaining wall, tearing off the car's front end, and Amick was instantly killed. Rathman won a second Indy race that afternoon, but it was shortened due to fear of another wreck.

In February of 1967, Curtis Turner sat on the pole in Daytona at just over 180 miles per hour.

NASCAR's 1965 Georgia State Sportsman Champion Aubrey Holley went to Daytona in '68, as green as could be, never having raced on a super speedway. The longest track he'd ever run was a one-mile dirt. According to Holley, he began making laps with the same type of engine Turner had used, running 183 miles per hour in his first ten laps. After he stopped, he walked over to his car owner, whose lips were quivering and hands were shaking.

The owner asked him if he'd ever been on a super speedway before. Holley answered no, but that he could go faster. The owner told him not to do it in no uncertain terms, saying he'd already broken the speedway record and scared the dickens out of him. Holley was well-known for his ability to set up a car, and, although he's not a heavy drinker, in his younger days he learned he could exchange his racing knowledge for a shot of good vodka.

Shortly after Daytona, Louie and Satch joined me, opening a new garage in Spartanburg. Louie was half a head taller than me, and he, Satch, and I had identical haircuts. When people ask me why I still have a crew cut, I tell them I have to wear it that way. It's constantly standing on end from jalapenos.

Louie was easy to get along with, smart, and well-liked by everybody. Good at anything mechanical, he could handle the engine, chassis, or parts, always figuring out how to make them work.

When we got together, we were a force to be reckoned with. We had to be good, with two wives and six children to support, and we got better and better finishes as we grew stronger.

I was running at Heidelberg, in Pittsburgh, near the end of the race, when I just gave out. A bowl-shaped quarter mile dirt track, its centrifugal force on my neck was so fierce I couldn't hold my head up to drive. Jim Reed managed to pass me on the 155th lap and won. I came in second, Lee Petty third, and Marvin Porter placed fourth. Determined not to be defeated by physics, I made a device with a bungee cord, fitting it under my arm and around my shoulder, to hold my head up to race. Later, I designed a harness with a strap that came down from my helmet, went around my left shoulder, and held my head straight. It saved me from working the muscles in my neck.

Another innovation was using a trailer to carry my car, which came about for safety and convenience. I got tired of towing my car on the ground and having to patch it to tow when it wrecked. I'd also been with Frankie Schneider when his car came loose and he lost it.

Frankie and I were in his family car going home from Sunbrock Speedway. His brother was driving a truck, towing the race car. We decided to stop at a restaurant to get something to eat. When his brother pulled into the parking lot, we looked behind his truck and saw the race car was gone.

We spent three hours searching, but it was nowhere to be found.

Finally, we noticed a set of tracks leading up to a sign, walked behind it, and there was the car. It had gone through at such speed, the sign flipped back into place.

Almost the same thing happened to Bob Flock. He was driving to a race with his wife when she suddenly commented that she saw a car going by just like his. When he turned to look, he saw it was his car.

A similar thing happened when Billy Carden was traveling with his crew and using a tow bar to pull his race car. He had made a stop and when they took off again, they noticed the car they were in suddenly had a lot more power. He looked back to see the race car, heading down the highway behind them on its own. When that happened to Charlie Mincey, his father was driving. They saw their car going by them. His father managed to get in front of it and let it catch up to them and then stopped it by gradually braking.

I started hauling my car on the trailer and it wasn't long before others followed, but, even with the trailers, disasters happened. Southern driver Eddie Spurling's trailer broke loose and his car ended up in a cow pasture. The farmer wouldn't let him leave without patching the fence.

Stan Starr and his wife Flo were in the NASCAR touring division and had an old school bus, still painted yellow. They turned the front part of it into a camper to cut down expenses, and carried their race car in the rear of it. They also carried another race car on a trailer hitched to the back. They rented the second car to racetrack promoters to put in their local hot shots.

114

It was a great situation. While they were traveling, Flo was in the front of the bus driving and Stan was in back, working on his car. There wasn't any roof, so the car stayed out in the wind and weather, as did Stan.

Once they were going down a two-lane road in Virginia when the trailer, with the second race car on it, came unhitched from the bus. Flo, who was driving, saw it go past them. The trailer kept on going until it reached a gas station, where it veered into the station's front window. Flo told Stan they'd better stop, but Stan said the people were probably mad and they'd better allow them a chance to cool down. Flo kept on driving until they came to another gas station and decided it was time to turn around. Neither one of them knew that the trailer's safety chains were dragging. When they went through the second station, the chains hooked onto the rubber hose that rung the bell to alert the station's owner a car was there. Those chains pulled up 200 feet of that bell hose.

As they went on back down the road, Stan told Flo the people in Virginia were awfully unfriendly, because they were chasing them when all they did was turn around.

Stan was later seriously injured in a race in New Jersey. Since he was completely covered by a body cast, his wife couldn't handle him alone. Singer and driver Marty Robbins sent his private airplane to take him home. With so many things going wrong, drivers had to rely on each other.

Marvin Porter always brought his wife and two kids with him. Like the rest of us, they'd sleep in their car, or on the ground, sometimes having to cook out in the open. That year, he moved his family near mine. He was broke, and I loaned him $150.

Years later, when neither of us was driving, he came from California, tracked me down, and paid me back. I've done a lot of good things for people, but I've had good things done for me, including help from the fans who'd visit my shop.

I roared to victory at Bowman Gray, Nashville, Asheville-Weaverville, and Martinsville that season. At Nashville, I was warming the car up when I broke the crankshaft. When I felt the vibration, I immediately pushed down the clutch to save the engine. Four more revolutions could have busted the block and ruined the pistons. We didn't have another engine, and if we'd blown that one, we'd have had to go home.

The Chevrolet dealership had a crankshaft and invited us over. They furnished a mechanic to help put it back, using the same pistons and rods, and the same bearings. We worked all night, and raced the next day. We always ran well at Nashville if we didn't crash.

I was especially proud of my win at Bowman Gray, where I shot ahead at the start and maintained my lead for all of its 200 laps. My wins there weren't always easy. During one event, Lee Petty led most of the race.

Lee was a rough-and-tumble driver, and would bang on you to let you know he was there. I tried to get by him, but he blocked me again and again. Near the end I bumped him, and his car flew over the guardrail. Meanwhile, I won the race.

Of all the drivers I'd run with, I admired Lee the most, watching and copying his moves, and learning a lot from the Petty operation. I remembered him telling me, "When you drive for money on short tracks, you've got to play as rough as the roughest."

I knew he wouldn't be happy knowing I'd applied that advice to him.

After the race ended, I walked over to him, stood as tall as I could and looked him straight in the eye. That wasn't easy with Lee at six feet and 200 pounds. I'd once told him, "When I'm in that race car, I'm as big as you are," but standing beside him, at five feet four inches, that wasn't the case.

For a moment we locked eyes, not saying a word.

"I ought to spank you, but I had it coming," he said and grinned, then he reached out and shook my hand.

I thought I'd handled the situation, when one of his angry fans walked over, punched me in the mouth, and broke my jaw. For six weeks, I was sucking my food through a straw. My talking wasn't so good either.

One of the most interesting events for me was the Darlington 500, but not because of my racing. I placed 17th due to a problem with my mid-shift bearing. The race was exciting because Rory Calhoun was there for *Thunder In Carolina*.

Fireball Roberts sat on the pole. Fans were, as usual, betting on how many laps drivers would go, but this time there was a film crew, panning the crowd and using the race as background.

Speedway scenes were filmed at Darlington and dirt scenes in Hartsville. I was paid for both. My car still goes round and round in that movie, which many die-hard fans own, but much of it's not realistic.

Joe Weatherly and I told the crew their "pit" terminology was off, but they wouldn't listen. There are a lot of things in that movie that are inaccurate. They should've hired an expert who knew racing language, but there aren't many good racing movies, especially about the old days. Few have made any money. If they made a real one, or as Ned Jarrett says, an "authentic" one, it would sell.

Race drivers were often asked to showcase their skills in action movies and they frequently flirted with danger. The early Hell Drivers appeared in a James Bond movie. Racer Charlie Mincey was a stunt driver in *Corky*, starring

Robert Blake, doing the racing scenes and some of the highway driving. His daredevil skills were so thrilling, he was offered a job but he wouldn't leave Georgia.

The winner of the Darlington race was Lee Petty, followed by Johnny Beauchamp and Charlie Griffith. Fireball trailed in the back with engine problems.

Darlington was famous for racing, and for "dunkin'." A lot of drivers stayed at the Holiday Inn, where they held wild pool parties. They'd throw in unsuspecting victims, especially girls. One night, the security guard was thrown in, gun and all. Partying and drinking were a part of the racing world for drivers and fans. It wasn't unusual for drivers to run with hangovers.

In '59, I started only 23 races, but roared to 5 wins, 11 top fives, and 13 top tens. In spite of this, racing rarely paid for building and maintaining the car. I didn't have full-time sponsors, only a dealer, here and there, and sometimes an ad. The ads went from $100 to $150. I took in about $12,000, but I was struggling. The money was barely enough to survive.

We knocked around that season, running our shop in Spartanburg. Satch, firm in his loyalty, stayed with us. He accompanied us to California chasing points. My main reason for going was to beat Marvin Porter, my rival in the Short Track Division, but in the last race I broke a ball joint, and failed to finish.

We ran all the races we could, running well, and chasing points, until the end of the season. Porter beat me by seven.

That winter, I built a race car for Monroe Shook and a '60 Chevrolet for myself. By that time, stock car racing had spread to South America. A guy from Peru was racing Grand National in Daytona, and Jim Rathman was racing in Peru. I got a call from a guy in Lima, wanting to buy a race car. Jim had given him my phone number.

I agreed to sell him my '59. He said he'd pay $3,500 for it, ready to race, if I'd put it on a boat in New Orleans. Mario Rossi, a mechanic, was in between jobs and rode with me in a tow truck to deliver it.

We were driving at night and he fell asleep at the wheel, running off an embankment. Both the car and the tow truck were wrecked, and we took them to Cuba, Mississippi, for repairs. I bought another '59 car without body damage for the guy from Peru, then took parts off of mine and put them on his.

The buyer was flying from Lima to New Orleans, where he was to meet us, but the plane crashed in Lake Ponchetrain, with no survivors, bringing a tragic end to our business agreement.

Louie Clements joined Mario and me to help get the cars back to Spartanburg.

117

Rex White with his daughter Brenda. "Brenda loved racing and liked to join me in the winner's circle. Kids weren't allowed in the pits until after the race. When it was over she'd come running in, her legs moving as fast as pistons." (Courtesy Motorsports Images and Archives.)

Back home, we switched parts to make a new race car for the '60 season. I kept two, a '59 and a '60, and moved Edith and Brenda, who by this time was four, down to join us.

They went to nearly all of my races when they were near home.

Brenda loved racing and liked to join me in the winner's circle. Kids weren't allowed in the pits until after the race. When it was over she'd come running in, her legs moving as fast as pistons. When I had money, I'd take her to her favorite restaurant, the one with the Golden Arches. It was also listed as a favorite by Satch, who 'til this day claims I starved him, and that drivers invented diets.

Racing is hard on families, and mine was no exception. Some people think drivers are heroes; I say it's the wives in the stands. For me racing came first,

Richard Petty with Rex White at an Atlanta Motor Speedway event in 2002. (Courtesy Anne Jones Photo Collection.)

and Edith and Brenda just tagged along. Their life was grueling, and in looking back, I know that was wrong. I should have spent more time with my wife and child. That's the truth and my biggest regret.

Later that season, I told Louie I wanted a gold race car. He mixed clear enamel with gold dust for a unique shiny shade. From then on, Louie would paint the car and I'd mess it up; then, he'd have to paint it again. That color became my trademark, although I have no big preference in cars. Some drivers get attached, but I saw mine as a piece of machinery. They all make fond memories when you win in them.

That year marked the last of the Short Track Division. Marvin Porter beat me, and I came in second. I was ranked 36 places higher than him, in Grand National, sitting on the pole 14 times, and winning 3 races. I came in 10th in Final Point Standings, and Lee Petty took first. He claimed almost $50,000 in prize money, and a third National Championship. His son Richard was Rookie of the Year, and one of his biggest competitors.

12

Sex and
the Super Speedways
Motorsports Gain Media Attention

"Jack Smith was running wide open. He finally knocked a leak in his gas tank and lost his fuel. I won by dodging the holes. You had to beat the race-track, just like today."

JOE LEE JOHNSON (Inaugural Winner, "Charlotte World 600")

1960.

Most media coverage had been limited to shocking and spectacular accidents, but in 1960, racing events were televised. Both the *Today Show* and *CBS Sports Spectacular* featured races.

Usually the media draws fans to a sport, but in motorsports, the fans brought the media to racing, and the super speedways fueled the nation's attention.

Another attention-getter was a super sex symbol named Linda Vaughn. Winner of the year's Miss Atlanta Raceway, Linda was breathtakingly gorgeous, and created a stir each time she visited southern tracks in the Atlanta pace car.

The next year she won a contest sponsored by the Pure Oil Company and became Miss Firebird, a position she kept for almost four years. The first time she appeared as Miss Firebird, she wore a bathing suit covered with sequins in red, white and blue. Amply endowed, she balanced atop a huge red bird, wings spread open and back, on a trailer pulled by a convertible. Linda, an instant hit with drivers and fans, became one of the most recognizable personalities in the sport.

She next became Miss Hurst Golden Shifter, a prominent participant at major motorsports and automotive events, where she could be seen waving from her standing perch on the back of an Oldsmobile convertible fitted with a replica of an eight-foot shifter. She later hosted the *World of Speed* on ESPN, made appearances in films such as *Gumball Rally* and *Stoker Ace*, and became a successful public relations professional. Linda Vaughn is now a major consultant and spokesperson for Prolong Super Lubricants and still frequents racetracks, lending an elegant touch to festivities as one of America's icons. Even today, old-timers, including myself, catch their breath when they hear her name.

In 1960 I jumped on the advertising bandwagon, continuing to use my car as a moving signboard. Piedmont Friendly Chevrolet, in Concord, North Carolina, offered me the use of a truck for a year, and $1,000 to put their logo on the truck and my cars. I quickly accepted their offer. They gave me tremendous support in my racing. If it hadn't been for their help, I couldn't have gone so far, especially maintaining two cars.

You can change from dirt to asphalt easier than asphalt to dirt, and it's hard to keep adjusting a car for both. We ran one of our cars on dirt short tracks, the other on super speedways. Having two made it easier.

In those days, when you weren't running dirt, there was good visibility. You couldn't talk with your crew, but you could tell what was happening by watching the crowd. When everybody jumped up and screamed, there was probably a wreck.

Darlington had a scoreboard, as did some of the smaller tracks, but it was hard to look up long enough to read it. Our pit crews communicated with us by writing on a blackboard sign. We called those signs our billboards. A pretty good size, they could tell how many laps you ran, how many to go, your position, and where the other guy was.

We used a lot of hand signals. They'd point to the back to say you've got to pick up, a guy's coming after you, and they'd stretch their arms apart when you were ahead. Fireball Roberts used to flick his wrist and hold up a finger each time he passed, just to let his team know he was all right.

The fans didn't know it, but our most persuasive form of communication was the hammer, especially for changing attitudes. It was the one tool every driver had. Some would even threaten with a tire iron, or, if they were really mad, they'd snatch another driver right out of his car.

We always had rear axle trouble at Martinsville, because of the low gear ratio we pulled. During one race, my crew could see smoke, but I couldn't. Louie jumped on the pit wall, fanning his butt like it was on fire. Despite our

Martinsville in 1960. "Martinsville was my cup of tea; or let me make that my Bud-weiser. I liked it because I always ran well there." (Courtesy Motorsports Images and Archives.)

troubles, Martinsville was my cup of tea; or let me make that my Budweiser. I liked it because I always drove well there.

The season started in November of '59. I had added James Hylton and Wes Roark to Louie and Satch in my pit crew. I knew James because he lived across from Frankie Schneider's home in Tampa. He would later become a driver and almost win a Championship. Becoming more and more outspoken, he'd become famous for challenging NASCAR, as he tried to make positive changes in the sport.

Wes had been a mechanic for Marvin Porter, who'd moved to California. I couldn't afford another man, but Wes needed work, and I'd seen how more manpower helped the Pettys. A former Ford team mechanic, he was such a good businessman, within two weeks, he was saving us enough to pay his salary.

Later, I added Ken Miller and Dean "Goat" Hall as additional crew members. Slick Owens came on as bookkeeper. Even today, Slick is known to hold

Left to right: Rex White with Louie Clements and James Hylton. (Courtesy Motorsports Images and Archives.)

his money so tightly, it squeals as it passes through his fingers. He was a former Korean paratrooper and Golden Glove Boxer, and it's said he could knock you out three times, before you knew he'd swung. A former gofer for Cotton Owens, he had a lot of racing knowledge, and became an important part of our team. We've stayed close over the years, and visit track events together today.

On race days, Jerry Donald, Randolph Barnes, and Robin Peter, our scorer, also helped.

Louie Clements was crew chief and Wes made business decisions, with our input. Everyone had a right to his opinion. We held meetings and made decisions among ourselves. Since we were like a family, if anyone had a problem, all of us chipped in to help. During our meetings, we decided to go for the Championship.

Looking after every detail, as was our policy, we didn't take anything for granted. Our strategy was to win through hard work and planning. We kept our garage immaculate, believing if you can't find something, you don't have it. I was teased about my garage because I'd painted the floor and it was so clean you could eat off it. Displaying our spirit for others to see, on race day, our crew dressed in uniforms.

The first race was on a half-mile dirt track at Charlotte. During the 124th lap, the horrified crowd watched Scotty Cain's T-Bird burst into flames on the backstretch. It took ten minutes to put out the fire, but the California driver was not seriously injured.

Buck Baker had sat on the pole, but came in third, after a wreck with Richard Petty. Jack Smith won the race, and I came in fourteenth.

I missed the second Grand National at Columbia Speedway, and we started the new year with Daytona. During the first qualifier, Tommy Irwin, another driver crippled by polio, spun out of control, across the grass, and into Lake Lloyd. Unable to swim, he climbed out of the car and onto its roof, where he was saved. Later, after several other cars took a dunking, that area was banked.

We ran in the second qualifier, where I came in fourth, and our mascot, Herman the "Turtle," was black-flagged. During the race he forgot his "shell," and was called out for not wearing a helmet. He got it in time to place 32nd in the 500.

Herman Beam was a legend in the old days. Always considered the underdog, he loved to run every race and got a lot of publicity. A one-man driver and pit crew, he was called "Turtle" for running so slowly. He stayed out of other drivers' way, always finishing in the back of the field, just hanging in for the love of the sport.

Because stock car racing was growing in popularity, NASCAR winnings, lap money and point funds were also growing and made it possible for the "little guy" to earn a living in racing. Herman Beam's consistency in putting finishing ahead of speed enabled him to rack up an astounding number of points for Final Point Standings. In 1961, he finished with 11,832, placing in 15th position, ahead of Ralph Earnhardt, Fred Lorenzen, Cotton Owens, Tiny Lund, Elmo Langley and over 100 other drivers who were contenders that year.

Herman, a chemist who graduated from the University of North Carolina, worked for Eastman Kodak in Johnson City, Tennessee, and like most of us, he started on the dirt tracks. Gradually he moved up to the super speedways, but never felt confident enough to play with the big guys.

Alex Gabbard tells the story of Herman finding himself, to his horror, on pole position at Hickory. That race positioned the slowest cars first, putting him out in front. When the pace car pulled off and into the pits, Herman went in right behind it. After the other cars thundered by, he pulled back onto the track.

125

Because he used his town car for his race car, Herman's car was plush compared to the rest of ours, having its complete interior. Leery of score-keepers, he recorded each lap on a notepad strapped to his leg. His wife served as his crew chief and when he pitted he'd jump out of his car to help her. In a big race, he might also have the assistance of a buddy or two. As the other cars roared past, race announcers would always add, "and there goes Turtle Beam." He claimed he didn't have driving talent but he was meticulous about his cars, keeping them in top shape and avoiding scrapes. Although he never won, his strategy saw him through over 200 races. It all goes back to that lesson I learned as a child. Set your pace, get in a groove, and you'll get the job done.

Saturday, the day after we'd qualified, we were in Daytona's pits during a Modified and Sportsman race. Over seventy cars were running, a lot of cars for a track. Within the first few minutes, a car went out of control, starting a multi-car crash. Although no one was seriously hurt, it knocked out a third of the cars. There were also horrifying wrecks during Daytona's Sunday 500 due to high winds blowing in from the beach. Tommy Herbert crashed into the guardrail and flipped, sending the front end into the air and destroying his car. Avoiding that wreck, Pappy Crane spun and flipped his car. Tom Pistone then lost control of his car and hit the wall. George Green wrecked, then his fuel tank burst and his car caught on fire. Bobby Johns would have won, but his back glass blew out and he spun, the delay giving the race to Junior Johnson. Fred Lorenzen floored his car to second and I finished ninth, all of this happening at an average speed of 124 miles per hour. At the end of the race, I felt like I'd been in a Hell Drivers show.

Nicknamed "Golden Boy," Fred Lorenzen came from Illinois, where he began racing Modifieds at Soldier Field and had instant success. The Yankee import was a smart businessman, often seen at the track with his briefcase. Known for always thinking, he had his mind in gear for winning, and the resources to do it. He downplayed his stardom by referring to "luck," but earned his way to the top through tough driving skills. Lorenzen had the charisma and looks of a movie star, and the press ate it up.

The fans ate it up too when they saw him drive. He claimed 26 NASCAR Winston Cup wins in 158 starts, sitting on 33 poles, with 75 top-five finishes. He became one of the top Ford drivers, representing the Holman-Moody team in the sixties, and was voted one of NASCAR's Top 50 Drivers.

While in Daytona, I met a character from California named Marchbanks. Everywhere he went, he wore a cowboy hat and boots. He'd come from California to get drivers to run his new track in Hanford. Joe Weatherly and I agreed, making plans to go in June.

Louie Clements (outside car) and Rex White at a pit stop in Daytona. "We kept all of our windows in at Daytona to make the car more aerodynamic." (Courtesy Motorsports Images and Archives.)

Because so many crashes had occurred in Daytona, NASCAR cancelled the following two Grand National races. Our next one was back at the half-mile dirt track at Charlotte Fairgrounds. Lee Petty sat on the pole. I grabbed the lead, but Petty bumped me, almost spinning me. That cleared the way for his son Richard, who took his first Grand National win, leaving me placing second. It was a generous gesture from Lee, who would do almost anything for position. He had challenged one of Richard's first-place wins and the rescoring gave Lee the race. It would help to make up for it.

Our competition resumed at North Wilkesboro, where Lee spun Junior Johnson from the lead to take first. Petty faced unhappy fans after the race. Angry at their homeboy's treatment, they hit him with rocks, bottles, and anything else they found handy. I was out of the furor, being a homeboy myself and having come in second, near my own hometown.

127

Many of us skipped the race in Arizona, because it was too far to travel with so little time. We went to Columbia Speedway for our next event. The car was running well and so was I, all the way to the bank. Buck Baker placed second, also running a '60 Chevrolet. He was followed by pole winner Doug Yates, who came in third, in a Plymouth. Because his family ran a Plymouth dealership, that was all he raced. It was my first win of the season and an omen of things to come.

The next week we were at Martinsville, Glen Wood's territory. Glen and his mechanic brother, Leonard, were a tight-knit team. They were dominant in Virginia and the Carolinas before their Grand National racing, and were very particular about their cars. When they got one set up, they didn't want anyone else to touch it and astounded drivers and fans by their super-fast pits.

Once, when Marvin Panch was driving for them they raced at Riverside, stopping at a truck stop in Greenville on their way back. They were in a truck, pulling the race car, which was tied down on a trailer behind them.

After they ate, they got on the road again. All of a sudden, they heard the most gosh-awful noise you could imagine. It sounded like a 727 aircraft was landing on top of them.

The noise kept on, so they pulled over and walked to the back of the truck. To their horror, they found a drunk, in Marvin's helmet, revving the race car's engine. When he saw them, he yelled for them to come on and win the race.

No matter how you look at it, that truck beat him. He was always a half length behind.

Alcohol is usually responsible for the most colorful racing stories. One time when a driver had been drinking, his wife hid his shoes, thinking he wouldn't leave their motel room without them; but, sure enough, he disappeared. The next morning he came back with a new pair, a brand-new suit, and two fifths of liquor. 'Til this day, no one's figured out where he got them.

One driver was so drunk at the track, a friend took over the driving, then immediately knocked down a utility pole. A highway patrolman was going to arrest him for DUI when another friend offered the officer white lightning to forget about it.

A fan once got so drunk he lost a company car. Fearing he'd be fired, he called the police and reported it stolen, hoping they'd find it. When they came, they pointed out the window and said it was in the parking lot. A quick-thinking fellow, he said, "Dang, it musta been kids. They got so scared they returned it."

Race drivers' main concern was dealing with fire, but to some fans, it became a friend. On cold nights before a race, they'd get drunk, then get warm by burning their beer cases near where they slept in the trunk of their car in

128

the infield. A 1960 Bonneville's trunk was so big two guys could stretch out and pull the lid down. A car slept as many as six, including seats and floors. In the morning, they paid with pounding heads and aching backs. Fan James Harper claims he knows this from experience.

At Martinsville, Glen Wood sat on the pole, but Richard Petty and Jim Massey zoomed past him, leaving me in fourth place. The win brought Richard to first in Final Point Standings, an honor I was determined would only be temporary.

On April 15th, we raced the Hickory four-tenths mile dirt track. I sat on the pole, but my rear end went out. I lost laps and dragged in 14th. In the following race at Wilson, Emanuel Zervakis sat on the pole. He came in first, but was quickly disqualified. I had built the car he was driving for Monroe Shook, but Emanuel had altered it. When NASCAR discovered an oversized fuel tank, his ouster gave Joe Weatherly first, Lee Petty second, and me third. Richard Petty trailed in seventh, but kept his Point Standings lead. Nicknamed the "Golden Greek," Zervakis would later become a car owner, after winning only 2 races in 83 starts.

At Bowman Gray Stadium in Winston-Salem, Glen Wood sat on the pole, led every lap, and won. I came in a fast second. This was followed by placing 9th at Greenville-Pickens due to rear end problems, and 7th at Asheville-Weaverville.

The Darlington Rebel 300 was a convertible race. I'd taken a hacksaw to my '59 Chevy, fixing it to run as hardtop or convertible. I wouldn't have bought a convertible if I could have afforded it, as a hardtop frame was lighter. I decided to run my '60 hardtop, as it was the better of the two and the race was a mix. The race was called after 74 laps due to rain. Afterwards, there was a week-long argument over how to restart it under the caution flag or the green, and one of the main protesters was Little Joe Weatherly.

On the day the race resumed, thousands of fans showed up with little green flags. Despite their outpouring of sentiment, it began under caution, allowing cars low on gas to pit, and hurting those who'd fueled. Pole-sitter Fireball Roberts made a quick stop and continued his lead. During the race Johnny Allen's car soared over a guardrail. It knocked down half of a scoring stand full of people. Scorer Morris Metcalfe was one of them. In spite of the drama, no one was badly injured. Johnny's car was torn all to heck, but he was okay. Fireball's A-Frame broke and Joe Weatherly won, ahead of Lee Petty's second, and my third.

Johnny Allen was a hard charger and a good driver, but he was known more for his crashes than his wins. Once, when I loaned him a racing engine because he was broke, he came in first with it in Atlanta.

We had to help each other because we were needy. I don't remember what it cost to run a season, and didn't write down expenses because they were always more than I had. I kept books by the feel of my left rear pocket. When there wasn't any money there, I knew I wasn't taking in enough.

I finished 12th at Spartanburg and 11th at Hillsboro, but gave Lee a fierce battle at Richmond. Ned Jarrett sat on the pole, but Lee and I soared ahead of him. Despite blowing a tire, Lee won and I came in second. It's amazing how many problems can happen and a driver still win. Cars have crossed the finish line sideways and backwards, and even flown across when the driver was hit from behind. Of course, the opposite also holds true. In his first race, Rubye Johnson's son didn't know he'd almost won when, having bumped another driver, he stopped to apologize. A fine southern gentleman, but inexperienced, he showed kindness that cost him the race, and gained him a nickname, "Gentleman Bob."

It was during 1960 that many of the drivers decided not to go to California, as the money was too little to warrant the trip. I'd promised Marchbanks I'd be in his inaugural race, and had signed the registration. Since he'd advertised my entry and Bill France was flying me out and back, I was committed to go.

Marchbanks was a racing enthusiast who owned thousands of acres in the middle of California. He'd graded a track right on his ranch in Hanford. Marchbanks Speedway was a mile and four-tenths super speedway dirt track. Located in the San Joaquin Valley, it was an isolated country racetrack, but its 250 milers increased Final Point Standings.

The track was good, considering it was dirt, but there was little hope for its survival. It had few grandstands, outhouse toilets, and unbearable heat, which contributed to high levels of carbon monoxide. It went over as well as La Cucaracha in a punch bowl. Race day was 104 degrees. My rival Marvin Porter won, followed by Joe Weatherly. I came in 8th.

Marchbanks was more successful at his "Cowboy Barbecue," and perhaps should have opened a restaurant. He got a front-end loader, dug a hole in the ground, added an air tunnel, built a fire in the hole, and put timbers over the fire. He let it burn down to coals and added mesquite. Then, he lowered a dead skinned cow onto the timbers, and covered the whole thing over with dirt. It cooked for twenty-four hours.

When he took that cow out, he cut away the dirty part of the meat and served it to fans.

I ate some myself, and I'll tell you, it was good. Joe Weatherly was there, but refused, having seen the po' skint cow lowered.

130

13

Chasing the Championship
Against the Giants

"The reason I'm in racing now is because of heroes like Rex White. He helped lay the foundation for what NASCAR is today, and inspired me to pursue a profession in motorsports."

ED CLARK (President, Atlanta Motor Speedway)

During the rest of the 1960 season, I continued to travel back and forth to California. On planes, I was usually mistaken for George Gobel, an actor similar to me in looks and size. I'd just go ahead and sign his name for an autograph, never revealing my identity. On one of my West Coast trips, I sat by singer Fats Domino. We exchanged autographs, and I had him sign a dollar.

On one California trip, I was cited for speeding. I protested, telling the judge I hadn't seen a speed limit posted for miles. I told him I'd asked at a gas station, but the attendant didn't know either. I said a state as big as California should be able to afford more signs. The judge shook his head, gave up the fight, and gave me my money back.

Later, I got in trouble, making national news when I had difficulty renewing my driver's license. The real story involved plans for racing, in New York and Montreal. I had to have a proper license, tags and insurance. Since I was living in Spartanburg, with a Maryland license and plates, I went to the Highway Department to get my license changed over. The first thing I was told was to take a driver's test.

During the test, I parallel parked and drove away from the curve without

131

giving a hand signal. The examiner made a smart-aleck remark, and I shot back, "Whaddya think mirrors are for?"

He told me to drive around the course, and do an immediate emergency stop. I did, throwing him into the dash so hard he dented it. To get his revenge, he flunked me.

The next day, I went back, controlled my temper, and passed. At my shop, Jim Foster, Sports Editor at the *Spartanburg Herald Journal*, overheard the story. He gave it to the Associated Press and it went nationwide. Hundreds of thousands of people, reading their papers, thought a top NASCAR competitor couldn't parallel park.

I got razzed about that a lot through the years, but I admit I get a laugh out if it myself.

It was still being discussed at the first World 600. Held at Charlotte Motor Speedway, the event was a wild scene of anger and confusion. The speedway wasn't ready in time for the race, and I was reprimanded for badmouthing the track in front of reporters.

It was still unfinished by the Grand National deadline. Its infield pits were filled with rocks and gravel, and there were no buildings or restrooms, just Port-a-Pots. The track's asphalt wasn't cured and holes opened up during the race, eight and ten feet wide. They were large enough to lose a car in.

All of the cars were battered by rocks. We put shields on their fronts to protect the radiators. I put three windshields on my car, but took one off when it became so shattered I couldn't see.

Lee and Richard Petty, Junior Johnson, Paul Lewis, Lennie Page and Bob Welborn were all disqualified for cutting through the infield. They received no points, and no money. Fireball sat on the pole, but didn't finish. The winner was Joe Lee Johnson, followed by Johnny Beauchamp and Bobby Johns. The race was teeming with danger because the track was a terrible mess. The event took Richard out of the contest for Final Point Standings.

Charlotte is day and night different than Daytona and it's never been smooth. There's still rough paving, despite massive efforts to improve it. The track is a challenge, especially the "humpy-bumps" in turns one and two. I never won at Charlotte, but had some powerful runs, and took a second.

The next week, I placed third at Bowman Gray. Lee Petty sat on the pole, but came in second behind Glen Wood. Petty was known for being obsessed with winning. Once when he stopped his car to change tires, his son Richard climbed onto the hood to clean the windshield. Lee took off full blast, with Richard clinging to the car as screaming fans and NASCAR officials desperately signaled. He finally brought the car to a halt when the race was black-flagged.

Rex White and Joe Lee Johnson at a Georgia Automobile Racing Hall of Fame reunion in Chattanooga, Tennessee, in 2003. "Joe Lee won the first Charlotte World 600." (Courtesy Anne Jones Photo Collection.)

The second Daytona race of the season was held July 4th. Jack Smith sat on the pole and won after a fierce breakneck finish against Cotton Owens. David Pearson was in the race, too, driving a Chevrolet. I came in sixth, but strong enough for a Final Point lead.

I saw Cotton and David recently at the Piedmont Fairgrounds in Spartanburg, where fans had gathered for a race and reunion. It had rained for days and the track was so muddy, chunks of wet red clay pummeled cars and drivers. Cars wore protective screens and those with windshields made pit stops to clean them. There were two spectacular wrecks, but no one was seriously injured. One car got caught in the mud at such speed it suddenly stopped and flipped over frontward.

David Pearson had been forced into the wall during the feature the previous year and, itching for retribution, he'd spent months preparing his car. Staying far out in front of everyone, he roared into first place well ahead of the pack. The event brought back memories of days gone by. Our tales and jokes brought back memories too, gaining color in each retelling.

133

Top: "David Pearson had been forced into the wall the previous year and, itching for retribution, he'd spent months preparing his car." (Courtesy Anne Jones Photo Collection.) *Bottom:* left to right: David Pearson, Slick Owens, and Sidney Jones pose for the camera at the Piedmont Fairgrounds in Spartanburg. (Courtesy Anne Jones Photo Collection.)

David Pearson enjoys looking at racing memorabilia at J.B. Day's "Raymond Parks" Birthday Party in 2003. (Courtesy Eddie Samples Photo Collection.)

My next two 1960 races were wars waged against the Pettys. They worked as a team on the track against other drivers, and together were a serious threat. Lee zoomed into first in Heidelberg, where Richard came in second and I placed third. In Montgomery, New York, we reversed. I took first, with Richard following and Lee placing third.

Grand National racing was usually short of automobiles, especially in northern circuits, because most of the guys who raced were from the South, and many wouldn't go north to run. The promoters sometimes offered "deal" money as well as prize money to insure a full track, and they were glad to see us, as were the fans.

Drivers were as anxious as the promoters to get their cars on the tracks, sometimes resorting to outlandish antics. When driver Sam McQuagg flipped his car in a heat race in Jacksonville, his crew jacked his crushed roof back up in time for him to win the feature.

Once, Charlie Burnette tore up his transmission during warm-ups. He hired a wrecker to help swap the transmission out, but the announcer called, "Two minutes 'til time trials." Knowing there was no way they could swap the transmission that fast, he hooked the car to the tow truck, jumped in the cab and pulled the car around the track to qualify. Afterwards, he put the new transmission in and won the race.

Another time when Charlie was leading, he went around a curve and saw a gas tank. He laughed and made three more laps before realizing it was his. He put it back on with baling wire and still won the race.

Buck Baker won our next race in Myrtle Beach, speeding ahead of all of us. Lee placed second and I placed third, with Junior and Richard right on my tail. Although I didn't win, it raised my Point Standings to over 2,000 points above my nearest contender's, and raised my hopes of winning the Championship.

July marked the inaugural of the Atlanta International Raceway, later known as Atlanta Motor Speedway. The track had a good clean surface, with just a few humps, and wide twenty-four degree banking in its turns. It was scheduled to open in '59, but like most super speedway projects, was besieged with problems.

Atlanta International Raceway's opening marked the ending of Lakewood Speedway and took a lot of attention away from the famous Peach Bowl Speedway. The Peach Bowl, a quarter-mile paved flat track, was located in Atlanta's northern end. When it first opened, the crowd was so large, management was forced to close the gates and turn people away. Five hundred seats were added in the first season. I only raced there once, but a lot of famous drivers were there many times, including the Flocks, Red Byron, and Tex Keene.

One time Tex was running the time trials and slid into a curve. Mud shot up and into the grandstand, ruining fan Rubye Burgess' dress. After the race, she charged straight for him, fuming. In spite of the situation, Tex was impressed. He asked for a formal introduction, and you can guess the rest of the story. Within months they were married at the Speedway. The Peach Bowl became known for wild events and personalities. One of the female drivers was Miss Ann Wesley, who was also a lion-tamer.

During the Atlanta race, I blew a tire and spun, ending my chances of winning. Our next race was the Dixie Speedway, a half-mile dirt track in Birmingham. Ned Jarrett sat on the pole, took on the Pettys, and won. The event was unusual in that no laps were run under caution. Of course, fans prefer that. We'd all rather see green than yellow, and the race goes by faster. Everything's about speed.

Our days passed in a blur of exhaustion and continuous activity. We'd stay up all night working on the car, then head for the track. I'd battle it out with the same guys we'd just faced before:

Fireball Roberts
Junior Johnson
Richard and Lee Petty
Ned Jarrett
David Pearson
Fred Lorenzen
Jack Smith
Tiny Lund
Joe Weatherly

Heavy chargers, their names were burned into those tracks and haunt them today.

I studied their cars and their moves until I knew them as if they were brothers, and it became that type of rivalry, intense and unrelenting. Yet, if something happened to one of us, the others were there. I can't tell you how many times I've set up guys' cars to see them beat me on the track the next day, but they were there for me, as were the fans who came to our garage. They searched for parts, helped with the lifting, did anything they could during those backbreaking days of working and racing, working and racing, working and racing.

Rex White and Louie Clements (right) display their trophy. "When we finished well, we ate well, and if we didn't, we put that page behind us." (Courtesy Motorsports Images and Archives.)

During a race, the only thoughts I had were of winning and preserving the car. We couldn't afford to risk everything to place because the car was our livelihood. When we finished well, we ate well, and if we didn't, we put that page behind us.

Nashville, Asheville-Weaverville, back to Spartanburg, Columbia, South Boston, and Bowman Gray. I had a good chance at the Championship, and we were hungry to win it.

Then there was Darlington.

September was the month of the Darlington Southern 500, and this one I'd never forget because of terrible tragedies. Fireball Roberts began on the pole. On his 25th lap, Elmo Langley crashed into the pits, injuring car owner

137

"The thing I loved best about racing was winning." Rex White receiving a trophy (the woman is unidentified). (Courtesy Motorsports Images and Archives.)

and mechanic Ankrum "Spook" Crawford, but that was only the start of the horror ahead. During my 95th lap I came out of turn two to find Bobby Johns's car upside down. Bobby was out of the car and his father was sitting on the pit wall. Not knowing what had happened, I continued the race. Later, I learned Bobby had tangled with another car, lost control and slid into the pit wall. The wall exploded, propelling a hail of pieces of concrete through the air. Mechanics Paul McDuffie and Charles Sweatlund were killed, along with NASCAR inspector Bill Taylor, assistant to Chief Inspector Norris Friel.

I hated that happened, for those killed and their families, and for Bobby and Socrates, his father. Believing the only way to succeed in racing was through physical fitness, Bobby was a driver-athlete who spent much of what spare time he had swimming and exercising. The rest of his time was spent in racing and with his father. Bobby and "Shorty," as his father was

Left to right: Rex White, Louie Clements and Perfect Circle Piston Ring Representative Gene Stonecipher admire one of Rex's many trophies. (Courtesy Motorsports Images and Archives.)

"I had a good chance at the Championship and we were hungry to win it." (Courtesy Motorsports Images and Archives.)

called, lived together, forming a close racing team. Sometimes they had pit helpers, but they generally worked alone. "Shorty" had been a midget car driver before going into racing with his son, and Bobby was known to have turned down a factory ride, when his father wasn't included.

I led part of the Darlington race, and was battling with Buck Baker, when he blew a tire. I took the checkered flag, but was told it was a scoring mistake. One of Buck's laps had been missed and he'd finished before me. There are disappointments in life, and this one was hard, especially for my pit crew. We lost what we had believed to be our first super speedway win. I heard my Father's words as if he were beside me, "Put that out of your mind. It's done. Now turn that page over. Don't talk about what's behind you. Say what you're gonna do." We choked back frustration and resumed racing at Hickory and Hillsboro. Hickory, haunted by the Darlington tragedies, had only 15 participants.

"At the end of the season, I claimed the Championship in Final Point Standings. I was voted Most Popular Driver and Stock Car Driver of the Year." (Courtesy Motorsports Images and Archives.)

I'd wanted to win at Darlington, but in the end my father was right. Instead of looking back, I should have looked forward. The points I earned during the race guaranteed my Grand National Championship.

Our days and nights ran together as time was ticking away toward the end of the season. In Virginia, Glen Wood's pole position was ruined by car trouble, and Lee and Richard Petty crashed into each other, sending both of them into the wall. The race turned into a war on wheels against Joe Weatherly, who was determined to beat me. We bumped and banged around the track, exchanging so much paint I thought my car's gold color had changed.

At Charlotte, the Speedway was rough, but vastly improved. Fireball sat on the pole, but a crash moved him back, and Speedy Thompson coasted to victory. Alfred "Speedy" Thompson was another driver who began on a shoestring, depending on friends for a lot of his help. He began his career on the

141

Left to right: Bill Wimble, Rex White, Johnny Roberts. "At the end of the season, I claimed the Championship in Final Point Standings. I was voted Most Popular Driver and Stock Car Driver of the Year." (Courtesy Motorsports Images and Archives.)

short tracks of North Carolina and Virginia. His sponsorship was limited to the painting of his car when Kiekhaefer discovered him. After Kiekhaefer withdrew, "Speedy" raced on his own until joining the Wood brothers. He won twenty Grand National races during his career, finally dying doing what he loved best, from a heart attack during a race at Charlotte Fairgrounds. But, in 1960, his winning streak continued at Richmond.

The grueling competition ended in Atlanta, where Bobby Johns barreled in first and Johnny Allen second, with the engine I'd loaned him. I placed fifth, with the Pettys pushing right behind me. Fireball sat on the pole, but his axle broke. He was known to floorboard a car until it crashed or died. As badly as I'd wanted that race, I was glad to see Bobby's win after such a hard season.

That year, we'd had a powerful, good-looking race car, and ran up front most of the time. I didn't end up in back, in the number four car, unless something went badly wrong. In most races, there wasn't any question where we'd start, and where we qualified generally indicated where we would place. When we qualified well, we outran everybody.

At the end of the season, I claimed the Championship in Final Point Standings. Almost 4,000 points ahead of second-place driver Richard Petty, I was voted Most Popular Driver and Stock Car Driver of the Year. We won more races, and received more recognition and write-ups than anybody. Nothing could equal our happiness. I may be short, but I felt tall and I was sitting on top of the world.

When we went to Daytona to be awarded the Championship, we were almost broke. Although my total earnings, including the Championship, were around $70,000.00, I'd used all of that maintaining our cars and feeding our families. I sold my 1959 car to driver-owner Jim Bray of Canada, to pay for our trip's expenses. I won the Championship with less paid out, laid out money, than any Championship ever won, and I was grateful. I'd had help from a bunch of people.

Because public relations was something I dreaded, and my most difficult obstacle, my next challenge was as big as a race. I had to dress right and speak to a crowd. First, I bought a suit for everyone on my payroll. Then, I took Bill Steel, Satch, and the crew to the Daytona End-of-Year Banquet. Most drivers just said "Thank you," but I acknowledged everyone, and Louie especially, because all of us won the Championship that magical season.

14

Hunting for Horsepower
Fighting Pontiacs with a 348

"Rex was one of the top-notch drivers, especially on the short track, the half mile smaller track. He dominated most of the races he ran. Drivers such as Rex made it hard to win. He was a unique driver and person and it was an honor to race with him. We could bang on each other on the track, then go down the road and eat together. Rex was that kind of guy."
JUNIOR JOHNSON (One of NASCAR's Top Fifty Drivers)

At the end of the season I took my trophies home to add to my mother's collection. Although she never went to a race, she was proud of me, and kept them in the living room, polished and shined. I was elated with my Championship, but a big track win eluded me and I was determined to have it.

In 1955 Chevrolet had come out with a V-8. In '55, '56, and '57 they had a top competitive engine, but success was short-lived. In 1958, '59, and '60, Pontiac was strongest. T-Birds could have been a threat, but their boxiness hindered their speed. Chevrolet was searching for a super performance machine, and I was searching with them.

Giving unofficial assistance in money and parts, Chevrolet helped drivers through local dealerships. During October, Chevrolet asked me to go to their General Motors Proving Grounds to test their engines and increase their horsepower. I took Louie Clements and James Hylton with me. Zora Arkus-Duntov, the famous Chevrolet engineer, supervised the project while testing the Corvette Stingray and its high performance small block 283.

Duntov, an immigrant with a heavy accent, was brilliant. He was born in

Belgium, raised in Russia and educated in Germany. Nicknamed "Zorro," he had driven in the Le Mans. In 1956, he scored a stock car record racing a Chevrolet at Pikes Peak, and set a world's record in a Corvette for the flying mile at Daytona Beach. Before coming to Chevrolet he'd designed overhead cams and valves on a flathead Ford, making it a powerful engine. At Chevrolet he was partly responsible for the 348. My testing showed the 348 to be low in horsepower and poor in performance despite its three two-barrel carburetors. It was a grave disappointment as I realized it was the engine I'd be racing with the next year.

You always remember the best places to eat, and a better part of the trip was the discovery of the Pinnacle Peak Patio Restaurant, a spot that began with old cattle drives from Tucson to Phoenix. Recommended by driver Mel Larson, it was my kind of place. If you dared go in with a necktie, they cut it off and nailed it to the rafters. Serving only pinto beans, steak, and bread, they cooked the steaks outside with mesquite, under the sky. The closest town was Scottsdale. We liked that restaurant so much, we went almost every night. It was our favorite place to go off the track and added another highlight to the year.

In the sixties, the super speedways changed the face of racing in the South. Dirt was still popular, but seldom were there more than one or two reporters for a short-track race. The speedways drew more crowds, more media attention, and added comfort. Their grandstands and food bars seemed luxurious.

Racing was luring more fans and respectability, but that didn't mean things were boring. There was never a dull moment at the track. We never knew what to expect, and there was always something eye-catching happening. Sometimes it was wild drivers and other times fans. The grandstands were dangerous due to drinking and rowdiness, and people were always spouting off and getting hurt. They were all operating on "asphalt." If a fight broke out, it was some other "ass's fault."

One drunk bet his friends he could cross a track before the cars got around it. He was wrong, and very lucky to have survived. In an incident rumored to have happened at Darlington, a drunk found his way back to his car, lay down inside and dangled his feet out the window, wiggling them against the side of another fan's car. By the time the second car's owner came out, his car's paint job was ruined. He went to his trunk, grabbed a baseball bat and broke the offending drunk's legs.

Driver Bobby Mitchell was known to take a nip in his younger days. One Sunday night, he decided to go to the drag strip after an afternoon of drinking. When his friends saw him, they immediately urged him to race. Bobby told them he wasn't racing because he was drinking, but they finally talked him into it and he lined up his Chevelle against a GTO.

146

The officials refused to let him run because he'd forgotten to take his hubcaps off, and since hubcaps can be dangerous, he had to get out and remove them. He remembers when they started the race, seeing that GTO in the distance, and thinking he'd better catch up to it. He'd been so inebriated when they'd lowered the green flag he'd forgotten to go.

Buddy Baker was badly banged up while racing at the Smokey Mountain Raceway, in Maryville, Tennessee. The infield exit was steep and as he was carried off the track in an ambulance, the back door flew open and his stretcher rolled out. Still under a caution, the cars came around a turn to find Buddy in the middle of the track. Thanks to the Gods of Thunder, they were going slowly. The ambulance driver loaded Buddy back in and away they sped to the hospital. After he was checked out, the ambulance driver asked him if he wanted a ride with him back to the race. Buddy said "Hell no," he'd take a taxi.

Sometimes events are funny and sometimes miraculous, and racing is no exception for those heavenly happenings. Southeastern Winston Racing Series Champion Ronnie Sanders was going down the straightaway wide open when the car in front of him spun. Just as Ronnie was about to barrel into the driver's side, the wind caught the car and lifted it upwards. Ronnie ran beneath it before it came down.

My biggest rival in the 1961 season was Ned Jarrett, and that's a fact. He came into the Grand National circuit in 1960, and ran the full season. We were the only ones who had a chance at the Championship, and ran side by side, race after race, waging war against Pontiac. It would sure as heck be a miracle, if I could beat him.

Known as a "Gentleman Driver," Ned always raced clean on the track. He'd jockey for position, but never knock you out of the way. He had a good personality and, wanting to improve himself, took Dale Carnegie courses. For years after he retired, he was a television commentator and his racing experience gave him insight helpful to fans.

The season opened in November at the Charlotte Fairgrounds. Dirt tracks always have surface problems, but this time, the roughness of the track took out more than half of the competitors, as car after car gave out. I was defeated by Joe Weatherly, and came in second, followed by pole sitter Lee Petty, Buck Baker, and David Pearson.

My next race was Daytona. During qualifying, Lee Petty and Johnny Beauchamp were in a spectacular crash, spinning both cars out and over the tunnel entrance. No fans were injured, but they came close. Both Lee and Johnny were hurt, Lee very badly. That crash signaled the end of Lee's driving career. Ironically, his son Richard wrecked in the other qualifier, flying over

147

"Southeastern Winston Cup Racing Champion Ronnie Sanders was going down the straightaway wide open when the car in front of him spun. Just as Ronnie was about to barrel into the driver's side, the wind caught the car and lifted it upwards. Ronnie ran beneath it before it came down." (Courtesy Anne Jones Photo Collection.)

the wall, almost to the adjoining Daytona Kennel Club. He wasn't seriously injured, nor was Junior Johnson, who was part of the tangle.

During the 500, Fireball Roberts sat on the pole in his Pontiac and had an enormous lead, but his engine blew and Marvin Panch won. Joe Weatherly and Paul Goldsmith came in second and third. Former USAC Champion Fred Lorenzen came in fourth. I finished twelfth behind Bob Welborn's Pontiac, and Jim Reed finished right behind me. Our underpowered 348 engine didn't have a chance. Pontiacs had all the horsepower, winning first, second and third places in the first qualifier; first, second and third in the second qualifier; and first, second and third in the Daytona 500.

The next race at Piedmont Interstate Fairgrounds' dirt track in Spartanburg was only two miles from our shop, and was the closest we ran all year. There were two Pontiacs in the race, driven by Cotton Owens and Junior Johnson. Cotton roared to first and Richard Petty slid in next, followed by David Pearson. Spartanburg was fast becoming a racing Mecca, as homegrown boys

148

set up shops and newcomers moved in from all over the country. There are still a heck of a lot of racing shops there today.

Again, the grueling blur of days continued as trying to win another championship, I chased points whenever I could, constantly adjusting and changing the car, not only for the tracks but to defeat the Pontiacs. I managed to fight them off at Asheville-Weaverville, although Cotton Owens and Junior Johnson were there. I sat on the pole, and then shot to first, followed by Cotton, Ned Jarrett, and Richard Petty.

Mr. Marchbanks, appreciative of my appearance at his track the previous year, paid for another trip to California. I drove a Ford in the race for Lloyd Dane, but was overcome by carbon monoxide. I took four hours to recover while a relief driver finished the race, despite a leaking exhaust. Fireball and his Pontiac were there and ready to roll. He sat on the pole, led every lap, and won. In spite of all our problems, I moved from ninth to fourth in the Final Point Standings.

Bob Burdick won the March Atlanta 500 in another bad Pontiac with me right behind him. I sped past Pontiac driver Ralph Earnhardt, who rocketed into third. When a problem with the scorecards placed me fourth, I charged into the scoring stand raising cane. I was promptly thrown out by Joe Epton, who later demanded to know what the argument was and said he'd fixed it.

Ralph Earnhardt was a heck of a driver, but he raced on as low a budget as I've ever seen. Like me, he had to be tough and race to win to support his car and family. I didn't begrudge him his place, but I was surely not going to accept being placed behind him.

In the old days, you had scorers to keep up with the race. At a hundred-mile event, NASCAR would find you one. In the smaller races, you'd better provide your own. Joe Epton was NASCAR's first and most famous scorer and Morris Metcalfe was a close second. Morris has the memory of a calculator. Never watching the drivers, he watched the scorers in the stands and could tell where every car was during the race. A remarkable individual, he'd score Bowman-Gray by himself. Fans knew him by sight, recognizing him by his white shirt and tie, and the 14 sharpened pencils in his pocket.

Scorers were assigned to each car. Often, one was a member of the driver's crew, and one was from NASCAR. Wives and girlfriends often kept score for their husbands from the officials' stand. Scorers would mark cards containing small squares for each lap completed, recording the time when their cars crossed the finish line.

The time was based on an electronically operated time clock, directly in front of the scoring stand. The clock would flip a card each second, from 1 to

149

9,999, beginning when the race started. The numbers were written in the squares for later reference along with pit stop delays.

NASCAR had men in the pits double-checking time, clocking cars as they came in for stops. For a long time, Darlington had the only scoreboard, and the first ones listed only five cars. It was changed only every ten laps, and the operator would get behind. I could be leading the race, yet be listed as fifth, then, boom, they'd change it.

In spite of the safeguards, there were often mistakes and uproarious protests, sometimes unresolved for days, and sometimes changing the winner.

It's always a good idea to have someone watching you. Elizabeth Petty watched the scoring for her husband Lee and spectators who volunteered to score could get back ticket money. A bunch of people helped score for me.

The most well-known track-worker couple was the Bruners. John Bruner was the Chief Track Steward and his wife Mary was in charge of credentials. If you sent in an entry, you sent it to the Bruners and if you paid at the track, you'd find Mary there. She also controlled the purse money, keeping cash in a suitcase to pay winning drivers. Drivers had to be able to collect cash, because they stayed away from home and on the road for long time periods.

David Pearson and I wrangled and spun at Greenville, but I recovered enough to place third. A sleeper, David sneaked up on us. He was a hotdog with a lot of talent, but it must have taken its toll. Premature gray hair brought him the nickname "The Silver Fox," and because of his early ability to take on big-name local track Goliaths, he was also called "Lil' David." Like me, he raced out of Spartanburg. Patterning much of his style after Joe Weatherly and Fireball Roberts, he proved himself a force to be reckoned with and eager to win, getting his start with Jack Purser and J. H. Watson, and eventually driving for Ray Fox, Cotton Owens, Dodge, Holman-Moody, and the Woods brothers.

The Pontiac war raged on in Greenville, Hillsboro and Bowman Gray, where I took the race from under the nose of pole sitter Glen Wood. Because Bowman Gray was also a football stadium, our most brightly lit night races were there. That was important, as many tracks' poor lighting caused wrecks and fatigue. Some tracks' electricity was so unreliable we had to finish racing in the dark. Hillsboro's one-mile dirt track was dusty and full of holes. It has now been converted into a state park.

I sat on the pole in Martinsville, but Fred Lorenzen pushed past me to win. By then, he was driving for Holman Moody, Ford's unofficial factory team. Glen Wood placed after me, then Zervakis. North Wilkesboro wasn't even a battle. Sitting again on the pole, I fought off Curtis Turner, Tommy Irwin, Richard Petty and Fireball Roberts to take the win with a two-lap lead.

I came in fourth at Columbia Speedway. Black driver Wendell Scott, from Danville, Virginia, was in the race, but crashed. He was a determined driver, with a low budget, and no sponsorship. Since he drove a Chevrolet, I gave him fenders, hoods, and engine parts when I could.

Wendell, a racing fanatic, started like me without any money. Even when his car had no chance of winning, he worked hard with support from his family. If his brakes went out in a race, he was running again in the next one. He didn't have horsepower, but he had willpower and as much enthusiasm as anyone. His wife, and all of his children, including his daughters, went to the track.

There was occasional, but limited, good luck. Once he was chosen to run a Chevrolet for Charlotte promoter Richard Howard, and another time he was given a year-old factory Ford. Wendell had to struggle all of his life. To go through the hardships he did to race was just unbelievable. Some people looked at his skin color. I looked at his character. A good person, well-liked, and helpful to other drivers, he drove in over 500 NASCAR events.

I once invited Wendell to our Spartanburg shop. We loaded all kinds of parts into his truck. He was in a lot of races with me, the first at Bowman Gray in '55. He finally won a Grand National at Jacksonville, Florida. The racetrack was rough, just a sandy soil track in a field.

Cotton Owens's Pontiac out-muscled me at Columbia, where Wendell crashed again. His car just couldn't hold up with so many used parts.

Junior Johnson's Pontiac outran me at Hickory, where Emanuel Zervakis scraped me before he flipped four times. The wreck was so dramatic it looked like a stunt, and the fans were hysterical. I'm sure they suspected we staged accidents for show, but the money wasn't enough to pay hospital bills or repair the race cars.

That's not to say drivers wouldn't show off or attempt to cover mistakes. One weekend, Bruce Brantley was racing in Newnan, Georgia, at a track with a high embankment serving as a guardrail. The dirt was wet and spectators were standing so close they were splattered with mud. Despite the mess, they were laughing and seemed to enjoy it.

When Bruce won the race, he remembered those fans, deciding to spray them once more with a victory lap. As he passed them, he slung his car into the turn, snagged the bank, and flipped the car over. The promoter immediately rushed to help and asked what had happened. Quick-thinking Bruce said he'd been offered big money for an exhibition.

Bruce was always having unusual things happen. Once, while going home from a race, he and his crew were riding in his pickup truck, pulling the race car, when they came across an old car sitting crossways in the road. The guy driving them locked down the brakes and as they skidded to a halt, a girl ran across the highway, hitting the truck's side. The impact spun her around and knocked her down. Afraid the girl might be badly hurt, Bruce and the others ran to her. Suddenly, she began screaming for her baby. Thinking an infant was lost along the roadside, they frantically began a search when they saw her grown-up "baby" boyfriend emerge from the darkness. Both were high as a southern pine and accused Bruce and his crew of reckless driving. It took the sheriff's department and the state patrol to finally sort things out.

Bruce started racing at age 14 when he borrowed his Dad's pickup truck and made donut turns in the church parking lot. But that didn't last very long. His Dad found out and put an end to his driving. Bruce was an expert at race car welding and later transferred his skills to a calmer environment, becoming a "shop" teacher in a metro Atlanta high school.

Most guys, like Bruce, got their start in racing at an early age in a family vehicle, but some got into it by accident. Russell Nelson was driving down I-75 to a race in Daytona with a bunch of friends when he came upon a wreck. He was driving too fast to stop, so he just ran into a ditch, came back out onto the road and kept on going. His friends asked him if he was scared and when he said no, they said he ought to race, and a star was born.

I placed third in the race at Hickory, but was elated because I was leading in points again. Then, the engine went out at Richmond. We were continually pushing the car to its limit and searching for horsepower. I began to think we were doomed when I sat on the pole at Martinsville and Junior Johnson floor-boarded around all of us to a four-lap victory. Junior, a former moonshiner, was known for being aggressive and rarely backed down. He'd trained on mountain roads outrunning revenuers. Later, he transferred his passion to car owning, and sponsored such greats as Cale Yarborough. He's led such a colorful life he's had a movie made about him. It's called *The Last American Hero* and stars Jeff Bridges.

My next race was the Darlington Rebel 300, which was a convertible race. Fans liked convertibles because they could peer into the cars and watch the drivers. I tried out a radio with a microphone, but it wasn't for racing, coming from an army surplus store and lacking noise cancellation. All my pit crew heard was the thundering roar of my engine.

Southern pit crew mechanic Jimmie Summerour had an unusual experience with his first racing radio. He was working for Johnny Allen when the first ones came out and he was anxious to try one. He couldn't contact his driver, but found himself talking to a lonely man in a logging camp in California. He told the man all about the race during their conversation.

Early race radios were unreliable and inconvenient, and they weighed about 150 pounds. Drivers had to choose between having no radio or having the extra weight in their cars.

152

Rex White during a pit stop. "Fans liked convertible races because they could peer into the cars and watch the drivers." (Courtesy Motorsports Images and Archives.)

Jimmie had another weird experience that nearly cost him his life. One night in 1954, he and the rest of the pit crew were driving home in Gober Sosebee's big Cadillac Coup de Ville, towing their race car. It was about three or four o'clock in the morning and Jimmie was taking a catnap, slumped down in the front seat with his knees on the dash. He was awakened to a horrific noise of the brakes locking down and the other guys screaming. When he opened his eyes he saw the tail of an airplane right over his head. He opened the door to get out, but Gober caught him by the pants and held him. If he hadn't, Jimmie would have fallen out and been killed because the car was going about 70 miles per hour. The plane had run out of fuel and the pilot, using Gober's headlights as a guide, had landed the plane on the highway in front of them. When they finally all came to a stop, they helped the pilot push the plane to the side of the road and waited with him until the state patrol came. When they started to get back in the car, Jimmie told the rest of the guys to go to sleep because he was driving and he wasn't going any further down that road with his eyes closed.

Jimmie got interested in racing as a kid, when he'd ride a streetcar to Lakewood Speedway. Later, he worked at the Peach Bowl, and from then on he was hooked. Once he got racing in his blood, he couldn't get it out.

To say racing is addictive is an understatement. Its pull is as strong as alcohol's, and I've seen it ruin as many marriages.

Coming off the number four corner in the Rebel 300, I tried to pass Bob Burdick when I hit his Pontiac, flinging my car into the inside guardrail and cutting my chin. While I was being patched, Fred Lorenzen and Curtis Turner slammed and banged into each other for 20 laps before Lorenzen finally passed Turner to win. It was a race that blended into a whirlwind of days, blurring work, travel, and speed, work, travel, and speed with my body fueled by adrenaline.

15

Battling with Brothers
A Rolling Racetrack Community

"He has the look of an athlete, specifically a top-flight jockey. There is a flat-top haircut, clear gray eyes, above average shoulders with arms like a middleweight, ending in powerful hands. Like most popular athletes, he has the faculty of putting people at ease and making them feel as if he is the one honored by the introduction."

RUSS CAITLIN (*Motor Life*, July, 1961)

The year 1961 was the year drivers almost got unionized. There was talk at the Charlotte Motor Speedway World 600. Curtis Turner was the main man behind it, with Tim Flock as spokesman. Tim approached me, painting a rosy picture of what the Teamsters' Union would do.

Supposedly, under the Federation of Professional Athletes, there would be bigger purses and a retirement plan, and drivers would have a voice in making the rules. I listened to what he said and planned to sign, but told him I'd think it over.

While I was thinking, Alf Knight and Ernie Moore explained the bad points. They thought it wasn't good to have the Teamsters in racing, and warned me not to get involved. That stopped my enthusiasm in a hurry. I backed off, deciding not to join.

Their advice was some of the best I've ever received. Para-mutual betting was being suggested, and would have brought corruption and ruined the sport. Bill France did well to foresee that scenario. Because of their involvement, he barred Curtis Turner and Tim Flock from NASCAR.

155

In response to the Union threat, a Grand National Advisory Board was formed. Ned Jarrett and I were on its panel and represented the drivers. We didn't accomplish much, but we did increase death and dismemberment benefits.

The World 600 was another '61 race dominated by Pontiacs. David Pearson won his first super speedway Grand National, followed by Fireball Roberts. I fought hard to keep third, fending off Ned Jarrett, Jim Paschal, and Tiny Lund. Pole sitter Richard Petty was defeated by engine problems.

There was a bad accident in the race, made worse by an improperly lapped guardrail. When Richard "Reds" Kagle's Ford blew a tire, it hit the rail, which sliced through the car and his leg. We ran a long time under the caution flag, as it was hard to get him out of the car and his leg was damaged so badly, it was amputated. I felt sorry for Reds, having known him, his brother, and their families when I raced in Maryland, but Reds didn't let that accident stop him. He continued to drive, performing well, especially in local races.

Jim Paschal won the next Grand National in a Pontiac at Piedmont, where I came in tenth due to engine problems. Jim had been in racing since NASCAR's beginnings, having run in the first NASCAR Strictly Stock race, and would eventually win two of the infamous Charlotte World 600s. Joe Weatherly sat on the pole, but crashed his Pontiac before the race was over. Second place was taken by Pontiac driver Cotton Owens.

At Birmingham and Greenville, I continued to battle the muscle cars, but I took Bowman Gray from Pontiac driver and pole sitter Junior Johnson, who came in third after New Yorker Jim Reed. It was an important event for me in the gold number four car, because the race was billed as the Myers Brothers Memorial. I thought highly of them, and they had been as close to me as brothers.

Southerners are known for adopting friends as relations, and the people who raced together over and over were like a family. We'd see each other again and again during each season, year after year. Junior Johnson's chief mechanic was Louie Clements's brother, Crawford, and that made sibling rivalry between us. Junior would bump you on the track and then go down the road and eat with you.

We fought on the dirt and asphalt, battling like brothers for every inch, but off the track it was different. We celebrated each other's wins and we suffered each other's pains. Side by side in pit stalls, restaurants, and motels, we were a mobile NASCAR community. Even now, it's somewhat that way, but they all have motor homes, costing hundreds of thousands of dollars.

I started on the pole in the "Yankee 500" at Norwood, Massachusetts, but Emanuel Zervakis won, again in Shook's car. I placed second, with Ned Jarrett and Buck Baker coming in behind me. Then there was Hartsville and Roanoke.

We'd race, make repairs, and then reset the car for the next track. When we were running well everything went right. When things went wrong we'd hustle, because time was everything.

At the race if something happened it was usually too late, and we ran the car as best we could despite the problems. When I won a race at Augusta with my car skipping, Louie worked all night to fix it so I could race again and win the next day.

A broken connecting rod threw me out of Daytona, and the Final Point Standings lead. David Pearson, Fred Lorenzen, and Jack Smith placed first, second, and third, followed by Marvin Panch and Fireball Roberts, all of them driving Pontiacs except for Lorenzen.

The upcoming Atlanta "Festival 250" was promoted to draw attention from a canceled USAC Indy race, when the Indianapolis track was declared unsafe. The event was marred by a spectacular wreck when David Pearson spun in his first lap. Although only three cars were taken out of the race, 12 were involved, and the track's wrecker flipped trying to help them. There were so many mechanical problems, almost half of the field didn't finish. Fred Lorenzen placed first in a Ford, and I came in tenth, but it was enough to be leading again in Final Point Standings.

That lead faltered, as I had engine problems at Columbia and Myrtle Beach. At Nashville, I was on the pole, but spun. Ned Jarrett, my nearest competitor, took over in Points. My lead had gone up and down like a Glen Echo roller coaster.

The next race was at Bristol. Known as "Thunder Valley" by fans, the track was between two mountains. Despite its small size, it has the steepest banking in NASCAR, but that banking didn't help me as my bad streak continued. There were a lot of engine problems again, and mine was one of them. It blew on the 285th lap.

I learned a lot from such experiences, such as not to rejoice until I got the checkered flag. Something can always happen, and races can be won by a foot, or an inch. The winner doesn't know if he's got a chance until he's out of turn four. Finally, I won again, at Bowman Gray.

At Asheville-Weaverville, the track surface began to disintegrate and we couldn't finish. The race was called early, with Junior Johnson placing first, Joe Weatherly second, me third, and Ned Jarrett fourth. The fans, upset over the loss of their money, rioted and blocked the infield. The drivers sent a spokesperson to calm them down but they wouldn't listen, and tossed him into an adjacent lake.

When a man tried to leave through the racetrack's fence, he was grabbed and beaten. Neither local police nor the State Patrol could break up the mob.

Hours passed as we were held hostage. People were hit, jabbed, and knifed, and several were hospitalized or arrested.

Big Maurice "Pop" Eargle, a huge man who was one of Bud Moore's pit crew, was trying to talk to the crowd, when a man with a two-by-four swung at him. He grabbed it and swung it back, slamming it against its owner. He then looked around and asked who was next. After seeing Pop's success with that two-by-four, the crowd dispersed. Pop, a former football tackle in high school, weighed between 250 and 300 pounds. He'd come to stock car racing after a stint with motorboat engines and midget cars.

The next super speedway race was at Darlington, where a Navy commander was in attendance with the Blue Angels. Johnny Bruner asked me to take him around the track, but to be careful with him. I took him around slowly, then at 100 miles an hour against the wall. We were so close he could reach out and touch it. He held onto the roll bars as if he would squeeze them in two, and I could see the veins in his hands as he clung for his life.

When we went back into the pits, he peeled himself out of the car, slowly regained his composure, and asked me if I wanted to go up with the Angels. I told him "Sure," and we headed for the airport in Florence.

They dressed me in a uniform and helmet and attached a chute, and away we flew. He put me through the drills they do in air shows, upside down, and all kinds of ways. We were going 150 miles per hour ground speed, when he pretended he was going to land, then pulled it straight up. It went to seven "Gs," pushing me so tightly against the back of the seat I thought I'd go through it. After we finally landed, he asked me if the experience had scared me. I told him no, I knew he wouldn't land going that fast because if he had, we'd have been in the next county. I was made an honorary member of the Blue Angels and given a special card and plaque for my bravery.

The following Saturday, I was getting ready to race when my car was disqualified over the way my engine was mounted. It had come that way from Chevrolet, and I'd been racing with it and was never told to change it. If I'd been told on Friday, rather than race day, I could have fixed it. I was angry and frustrated, having struggled so hard for my place in Final Point Standings.

Jack Smith had two cars, and when he found out what had happened to me he loaned me a Pontiac. Given a powerful engine at last, I tried to forget my bitterness, but the car didn't fit me and wasn't set up right. I couldn't adjust it to my size and foot, and driving was difficult because I was seated so far back from the wheel. Nelson Stacy won the race with Fireball, who sat on the pole, coming in second. Considering everything, I suppose I did well, dragging in 10th.

158

I sat on the pole at Hickory, ferociously battling Ned Jarrett as we continually swapped the lead. Finally his rear axle snapped and I thundered in first. I followed that with a third at Richmond, trying hard to catch and destroy his Final Point Standings.

Ned Jarrett won that year's Championship in spite of my efforts, and I came in second, only 830 points behind him. My crew and I had battled as many engine problems as we battled drivers, trying to add horsepower to our 348. Competing with the Pontiacs, we'd stretched the car and ourselves to the limit. We'd gone as far as we could, but it wasn't enough. When Louie Clements and I received *Motor Life*'s "Men of the Year" racing awards, it was a bittersweet exchange for the Championship.

16

Giddy-Up 409

The Dixie 400

"Rex was one of the best short track drivers I've ever seen. I remember his gold Chevrolet with its red number four. He was confident, knew how to set up his car, and was hard to beat. He was good on the chassis and his cars handled well. He was the man you'd have to outrun to win."

MARVIN PANCH (Voted Member of NASCAR's Top Fifty Drivers)

Right before the 1962 season started, I went back to the GM proving grounds. Chevrolet said they'd finally found horsepower, in the form of the 409 engine. I tested it in a '61 Chevrolet, and then in a '62. Supposed to be really powerful, it was more like a 409 paperweight.

We ran the engine in Arizona and Daytona. We'd go 168 mph in testing, but when we tried to race, we were slower. The '62 body style was less aerodynamic, but the engine just didn't have speed. The best use for that 409 was a boat anchor. We didn't want to admit it, but it was a fact. The drag racing people would differ, but I was racing ovals, and those engines were designed for trucks. They didn't have the horsepower to match Ford or Pontiac.

Back in Spartanburg, we prepared for the new season. Although Chevrolet wasn't my official sponsor, they supplied me with engines and parts. I built a new car for the 409, but there were lots of problems. We'd been running the 348 since '58 and were used to it, but now had to adapt the 409 to racing. The more we ran, the more we fell out. If it wasn't the engine, it was the rear end. Something was always going wrong, but when I could get through a race, I usually placed well or won.

I came in first at Asheville-Weaverville, Hillsboro, Richmond, and Bowman Gray, but I couldn't complete either North Wilkesboro or Greenville and crashed in the Darlington "Rebel 300," the second year in a row. We'd started with high hopes and a good race team, but my chance for another Championship soon disappeared. Disappointed, I turned away from chasing points and began chasing wins.

When you're chasing points, you race differently because you're more concerned with finishing than coming in first. You run harder when you're not chasing points, because it's more important to win, not just to finish.

I continued to alternate winning with engine trouble. I won at South Boston, Columbia, and Hickory, but had problems at Darlington, Martinsville and Charlotte. In '61, we'd run better with the more competitive 348, but overall my car handled well. Despite its problems, I'd sat on nine poles and won seven short-track races as the Atlanta Motor Speedway "Dixie 400" loomed ahead. Fireball ruled the super speedways. He and Joe Weatherly were two of my strongest Pontiac competitors, and I would have to defeat them both to have a chance to win.

The race was billed in local newspapers as a Ford and Pontiac contest, due to their manufacturers' rivalry. Leading Ford drivers were hotdogs Nelson Stacy and Fred Lorenzen, but the Pontiac competition was fierce. Fireball Roberts, Joe Weatherly, Bob Welborn, Jack Smith, Ralph Earnhardt, Jim Paschal, David Pearson and Bob Burdick were just some of the contenders I'd face.

The papers barely mentioned Chevrolet, briefly referring to Ned Jarrett and myself. Before the race, I was asked to pose for a picture with Tiny Lund that ran the next day under the headline, "The Little and the Big."

Atlanta was a lot different than Charlotte, although they're both a mile and a half, and close in size and banking. Atlanta has more turns than straightaway. It's changed some now, because it has doglegs. Doglegs are a D shape, and the backstretch is straight. The track has quarter mile straightaways and half mile turns that really get your car working hard. Its races are known for their wear and tear on tires and their unfavorable weather. You're almost expected to have a race delay due to rain.

Once when I was practicing at Atlanta, getting ready to set up my car, Al Smith was ahead of me. A member of Tiny Lund's pit crew, he would run the car for Tiny, and then set it up for him. I noticed every time he'd go into a curve, he'd almost lose control of the car, but worse, I just couldn't get around him. Determined to pass, I gave him a nudge to let him know I was there. When I finally got ahead of him, he was right on my tail, following only inches away through every turn. Later he said he was using me as his teacher to learn how to go through the curves.

Because I knew I could run lower in Atlanta's long turns, I felt certain I could place well, and my shocks were a part of my plan. When they're engineered right, shocks stabilize the race car by making it ride smoother and keeping it from yo-yoing.

We used to spend hours changing shocks and adjusting them for each race. Most people, even mechanics, don't understand shock absorbers. The only reason they're installed in a car is for rebound purposes and to keep the tire on the road. Nowadays, shocks are tested on a dynamometer. Ours were tested by trial and error, in other words just a good guess.

We went to Hampton, changing only the left front shock, increasing the rebound to cross the bump on the number one turn. Since it was in the middle of the racetrack's groove, it would hurt our lap time to go around it, but be a challenge to cross without upsetting the car's balance. Seconds meant everything and we had none to lose. I ran the softest spring I'd ever run on the left front wheel and although I didn't know it then, that shock would win the race for me, along with the shims I'd made for it from Coca-Cola cans.

I was 33 years old and had been racing for 9 years. My team, who were with me all season, had become a top-notch operation. When things went well, they performed like a well-oiled machine. Crew Chief Louie Clements was a mechanical engineering expert, and he could improvise. Louie'd take a piece of iron, beat something out of it for the race car, and not only make it work, but make the car win. He could do body work, paint, or anything else that needed doing. The only thing he couldn't do was electric welding.

Louie and I made decisions together on chassis. I decided whether to put in more bite or more sway bar, to have softer or stiffer springs, and to increase or lower the gear ratio. You always adjusted sway bars more on short racetracks. Every driver knew how to do the big things, but it was the little things that put you ahead.

My jack-man Slick Owens was faster than anyone, quick on his feet from his experience in Golden Glove boxing. Gas man Dean "Goat" Hall was a truck driver who worked as a volunteer. My other gas man, banker Jerry Donald, was also a volunteer. James Hylton, good in all positions, did everything. He'd eventually become a heck of a driver and car owner. His brother-in-law Buddy Payne also came when he could, and mechanic Don Bailey helped Louie with the engine.

My teams always worked well together. Everybody knew what to do and what was expected, and we were always pulling pranks at each other's expense. For instance, Louie was never a hard drinker, but he loved a good shot of white lightning. Once he got hold of a half gallon of "shine" that was especially good and he dearly loved it. We were working hard one night, and every so often, he'd go to that jar and take a shot. Slick couldn't help but notice and the devil got in him. He searched until he found a similar jar, filled it with water, walked back to where Louie was, and asked if he wanted another drink. Louie, of course, said yes, so Slick made like he was handing him the jar, then "accidentally" dropped it. If you could have seen Louie's face, as that water spread over the floor. Slick let him suffer almost an hour before bringing the real jar out.

Closeness was important to all of us, and racing teams were joined in friendship and purpose. The Woods brothers were the first to concentrate on rapid-fire pit stops, practicing at home in their shops. Their routine became so noticeable, others got wise to what they were doing and we all began to copy them. Because they were so fast, they were invited to pit for Jim Clark in an Indy race where Jim was to drive a Lotus chassis with a Ford engine. The announcer, Roger Ward, watched Jim come in for fuel and leave so fast he thought they hadn't had time to fill the tank. He told the audience he didn't know how the car could last the race. When Jim won, it astounded him. The win went down in history because it was the first rear engine win at Indianapolis.

One year my team won the pit crew race at Charlotte, having the fastest time of anyone there. Along with the money we won, we received a gold lug wrench. In the old days, a six person pit crew was big. Today, there are at least 15. Newscasters talk about the psychology that goes into building a team. In the old days we were thankful when people just "clicked."

The stands were packed for hours before the Atlanta race and drinking had begun the previous night. The Ford fans challenged the Chevrolets, saying the 409 couldn't win. The Pontiac fans yelled they'd win without a contest. Spectators were already betting on drivers, their number of laps, and cars. Then, hearing the deafening sound of engines catching, they rose to their feet.

Seventeen of the contenders would be voted among NASCAR's Fifty Greatest Drivers, and those Fords and Pontiacs were tough. Despite the competition, I qualified fifth, and was the only Chevrolet qualifying in the top ten.

Known for his daring, Fireball in his Pontiac sat on the pole and shot out like a bullet, leading the first three laps. Junior Johnson, also in a Pontiac, was hot on his tail, in an all-or-nothing attempt to get past him. Fans held their breath as on the fourth lap, he made it, grabbing the lead. Their battle fueled by adrenaline, they fought for another two laps before Fireball took over again and the crowd went wild.

Junior's efforts proved to be in vain. Car trouble took out seven drivers in the first 15 laps and he was among them. Lee Roy Yarbrough, Nelson Stacy,

Bobby Johns, and Tommy Irwin all had tires blow out, and smashed into the wall, thrilling the fans. Rookie H. B. Bailey flipped his Pontiac, but wasn't hurt. Twelve more drivers went out with breakdowns or crashes, adding more drama.

Joe Weatherly, Marvin Panch, Richard Petty, Fred Lorenzen and I kept our cars out of the fray and battled for position all day. One would surge ahead, only to be passed by another. I held back, wanting to stay close with the pack without risking my car, my tires, or my fuel. I knew the race was going to be won through skill and consistency and impatience could ruin me.

My pit stops went like clockwork, but after the last one, the race turned into a gas mileage contest, especially against Marvin Panch.

Marvin began his racing career as a car owner whose driver didn't show up for a race. He had been interested in racing since he was a child in California. As an adult he was a foreman at a brake and wheel alignment shop in San Francisco, where he loved watching open-wheel modifieds, now called roadsters, racing at Oakland Stadium. He attended one race during which he was fascinated by a driver who drove a six-cylinder against the V-8s. Impressed by the driver's smoothness and competitiveness, when he heard an announcement about an upcoming stock car race, Marvin decided to offer him the chance to drive for him. The driver asked Marvin what kind of car he had and Marvin took him out to the parking lot and showed him the car he was driving. They redid it into a race car and were very successful.

After a year, Marvin offered him a chance to run an old jalopy. The first night he ran it, he won the race backwards, having been caught in a terrifying spin as he crossed the finish line. He was so upset he said the other guys didn't know how to drive and he didn't want any more part of it. The next week, Marvin decided to run the car himself in a stock car race in Bay Meadows, a one-mile fairground track in Sacramento. West Coast NASCAR representative Margo Burke was there and suggested to Marvin that he become the car's regular driver and keep all the money he won for himself. That was in 1950. By the time of the 1962 Atlanta race, he'd become the first West Coast driver to be successful in NASCAR and had driven to a 1961 Daytona 500 win driving for Smokey Yunick.

In the Atlanta 400, Marvin became one of my most formidable foes. Known for hanging in when the going got tough, he had developed stamina by driving his passenger car with the air conditioning off and the windows up, and taking the steering belt off to drive it without power steering. He also had a seat at his house with a steering wheel designed to be hard to turn. When he'd sit to watch TV, he'd work that wheel back and forth to strengthen his muscles. Like me, he couldn't stand to wear gloves, and his hands were always covered in calluses.

Bill France, Sr. (tall man in center) congratulates Rex White (in helmet). From left to right in background: James Hylton, Louis Clements, Ken Miller, and Wes Roark look on. (Courtesy Motorsports Images and Archives.)

During the race, I watched him in his Wood Brothers Ford like a hawk eyeing prey. I conserved my fuel by constantly drafting, trying to make it to the end, with a deep-rooted memory of running out of gas in Birmingham.

"Poor Boy Roberts" had volunteered to help me in that race, as my gas man. We were leading when I pulled in to pit. As usual, we were using a can with a one-inch vent on the side to fill up the fuel tank. The gas man always put his thumb over the vent, to prevent spillage, until he could fit the neck of the can into the tank. Poor Boy was so excited he didn't release his thumb, and I sped away without getting a drop.

Since I was a dark horse in the Atlanta race, my pit crew tried to encourage me. Louie held up a sign saying "Giddy Up 409." Later in the race it was followed by another one, spelling G-A-S, followed by a question mark.

Marvin took the lead and I stayed on his bumper, drafting for close to a

From left to right: singer Feron Young, mechanic Louis Clements, driver Rex White, beauty queen Jean Phillips, and Jack Blair celebrate. "Winning the Atlanta Dixie 400 was an adrenaline high." (Courtesy Motorsports Images and Archives.)

hundred miles. Finally, with three laps to go, he ran out of fuel. I backed off my throttle fearing the same thing would happen to me, then sailed across the finish line, beating Joe Weatherly in his Bud Moore Pontiac by only 12 seconds. Marvin managed to get back in time to place third, followed by Richard Petty and Fred Lorenzen.

The stands were in an uproar as the Chevrolet fans went crazy, their noise drowning out the winding down of our engines. The Gods of Thunder smiled on me in the Dixie 400 and I was triumphant.

Winning was an adrenaline high more intense than the race. We didn't have a Winner's Circle, so we pulled to a celebration spot behind the pit wall. The beauty queen Jean Phillips gave me a kiss, and I met country singer Feron Young, a former paratrooper who had served with Slick and was Grand Marshall.

167

The next day, my picture was taken with Governor Vandiver as he presented me with my trophy at the capitol. The celebrating was a thrill for me, and meant even more to my fans. I'd been the underdog, and they'd pulled hard for that 409 engine. It would be the only super speedway race a 409 won, and the first major win for Chevrolet since Joe Lee Johnson's "World 600."

The season closed with Joe Weatherly winning the Final Point Standings. Spending the year as broke as my crew, he'd hitchhiked his way to victory, persuading owners to let him drive, especially in hundred milers. Sometimes he just showed up at the track and hunted a ride. The runner-up was Richard Petty, followed by Ned Jarrett and Jack Smith. I came in fifth. Our mascot, Herman Beam, who drove across the finish line last in Atlanta, ranked eleventh, shockingly outdoing the hotdogs such as Junior Johnson, Tiny Lund and Cotton Owens by just hanging in there.

Atlanta was a boost for my career, the longest event I won, and the grandest moment in racing for me—and for Chevrolet fans.

17

From Detroit to Despair
Chevrolet's Mystery Engine

"Rex White was the best short track driver that ever walked the earth. He blew everybody away."

FRED LORENZEN (Member NASCAR's Fifty Greatest Drivers,
Driver for Ford's Holman Moody Racing Team

NASCAR grew like a wildfire during 1962, acquiring more followers and more tracks. The attraction stock cars held had a tremendous effect on the fans, an effect clearly noted by automakers.

After the Atlanta "Dixie 400," Chevrolet was anxious to get back into racing. Excited about their new 427 engine, I went to Detroit to negotiate for one for Ray Fox and one for myself. Ray, a master mechanic, was behind many famous racing success stories. Fireball Roberts, Marvin Panch, Buck Baker, and David Pearson were just some of his drivers. I wanted each of us to have a '63 Chevrolet, and racing equipment. Ray wanted Junior Johnson as driver and I wanted my own racing team. I returned home hopeful of having it.

Several weeks later, I went back, taking Louie Clements with me. My efforts were rewarded with Chevrolet sponsorship again, although rather than have a factory team, Chevrolet chose to sponsor individual owners and drivers and I was proud to be one of them.

Louie and I built two '63 Chevrolets for the 427 and immediately took them, and our crew, to the proving grounds. The first thing I did when we arrived was take everyone to the Pinnacle Peak Patio Steakhouse. The only one disappointed was Slick, who'd rather have had a peanut-butter sandwich.

In racing, I was surrounded by unusual eaters. Satch Steel, always starving, would eat almost anything. Frankie Schneider was the fastest, and Slick was the oddest. He was known to upset waiters by ordering a green bean sandwich. Wherever we went, he filled our car trunk with crackers, usually of the peanut-butter variety. When we'd go to a steakhouse, he'd order tomato juice, which he'd treat like soup, filling it with crumbled saltines.

Ned Jarrett was a chocoholic who, in his early racing days, existed on cocoa and chocolate milk. His mother had raised him on chocolate gravy, which, according to Ned, is a mixture of flour, milk, butter, sugar, and chocolate, cooked in a frying pan until it boils, and then served on biscuits. I've tried that concoction, and I must say it's good. It reminds me of homemade chocolate pudding, but it can't compare with the food at the Pinnacle Peak Patio Steakhouse.

When it comes to eating, I can mostly take it or leave it, except for hot chili peppers. I discovered them in California and put them on everything but ice cream. Whenever I get too laid-back, they kick me to life.

Louie, Ken Miller, Slick, and I tested the 427 all through January and were excited to find Chevrolet finally had horsepower. Hearing the news, Junior Johnson came out, but refused to run after seeing the test track. The track's course was flat, with abrupt thirty-foot angled banking and no guardrails. Since a driver could fly out the sides and into the desert, one wrong move could have been his last.

Too happy to be afraid of the track, I continued to test, running 188 miles per hour with the 427 in my '63 Chevrolet. Driving the fastest I'd ever driven, I felt like I was flying, and set my personal driving record for speed that I still have today. Of course, speed is relative. It doesn't matter if you're going 5 miles per hour or 500 miles per hour. It's the competition you have that counts.

That 427 would run, but there was a problem. Its production was three months behind. Since we didn't have enough engines, we tested headers and exhaust pipes until we ran out of parts. With nothing left to do there, we went back to Spartanburg and set to work building a new car for Daytona. We had to take the cylinder heads off a 427 we'd blown and put them on the used one in our race car, but we had high hopes of being competitive. The car was ready to race, and I was pumped and ready to roll.

The power of the 427 was instantly noticed. Other drivers and car owners caught our excitement and since, in NASCAR, all engines have to be available to the public to be considered stock, Ford's Holman Moody demanded their own. Ray Fox and Junior Johnson had been waiting for it and received new cars with the 427 in them. Car owner Smokey Yunick had just switched from Pontiac to Chevrolet and was given one of the cars I'd built and tested for his driver Johnny Rutherford.

We were anxiously awaiting the Daytona 500 when, one week before the event, Chevrolet pulled out of racing again. Chevrolet had been involved only a few months, when GM was suddenly accused of becoming a monopoly. The company backed off from high performance to stop the threat of government intervention. They ended our operation and stopped producing replacement parts. We had an engine that could dominate, but couldn't maintain it. Their withdrawal left me stranded.

Despite my loyalty to Chevrolet, car owners with power and influence received first choice of the engines we'd tested and I wasn't given one. I had been revved up, only to be dropped like a bucket of lead. In Spartanburg, I'd built an addition to my shop and hired new employees, but it all went down the drain with Chevrolet's exit.

Feeling I'd been treated unjustly, I was furious. Angry and fed up, I felt as if I'd been kicked in the gut, the wind knocked out of me. It was one of the most painful letdown experiences of my life, and the blow that would end my career.

I wasn't a politician. I didn't dress well, talk well, or have flair. I didn't know even bad publicity's good, if they spell your name right. Unaware of the strategies of self-promotion, I took what I could get, which was what was left. Not knowing about public relations, I thought excellence was enough, but I was wrong.

Looking back, and looking at racing today, I see what politics can accomplish, and how playing the political game can make a difference. Today's drivers have to be able to race and meet the press. Darryl Waltrip, one of NASCAR's 50 all-time Legends, is an example. His driving seems natural, and self-promotion comes naturally too. The only five-time winner of the Charlotte Coca-Cola 600, he raced hard and knew how to win, but his nickname is "Jaws." He's such a good talker, you could tape up his mouth, leaving one corner open, and have an hour-long interview. I wasn't a talker and didn't know how to present myself. There are many things I know now I could have done to help my career. But, that's known as hindsight, and if I had to do it again, I might still forego the show, and come out the same.

Our trophies, important at the time, were just symbols of the things we accomplished. They looked good, but they didn't display our spirit, or the effort poured into attaining them. They were meaningless without the story behind them.

We worked long and hard, sacrificing all we had for what we believed we were meant to do. We achieved, for all the right reasons. We loved what we did and were good at it. Chevrolet didn't put me out of racing, but they made me choose. I could continue the exhausting, never-ending struggle, or I could stop. In the end, the effort would prove too much.

Disheartened, and believing I could have conquered any speedway with the right equipment, I swallowed my disappointment and prepared for the Daytona 500, reusing most of my parts, including head gaskets.

As usual we arrived early, as did many of the other contenders. Marvin Panch was there and decided to test Rick Cunningham's Maserati sports car. He was flying down the track when it went airborne, flipped out of control and landed upside down. Several onlookers, including Tiny Lund, sprang to his aid, lifting the car high enough for him to kick the door open. He was about halfway out when the gas tank blew up, knocking his rescuers back and forcing them to drop the car on him as it burst into flames. Seeing Marvin was still alive, they ran back into the flames, lifted the car again, grabbed Marvin by the legs and pulled him out. His clothes were already burning but he was able to roll on the ground and put out the fire. He and his rescuers were burned, but the rescuers were not burned badly. To this day, Marvin claims while he was trapped in the car, everything he did in his life, especially the things that were bad, passed before him. He says it was as clear as watching TV and caused him to stop and think, and to change his lifestyle. Gravely injured, but grateful to be alive, Marvin decided Tiny Lund, who was carless, should drive in his place in the Daytona 500.

I qualified well and the car ran so fast, it could have sucked the paint right off Tiny's car. I had the chance, and the engine, for another super speedway win when, running hot, I blew a head gasket. I stopped, got water, then tore back into the lead, but had to stop when I ran hot again. Twice obtaining the lead, I'd led 26 laps of the race when, in spite of my efforts, Tiny Lund won, rolling under the checkered flag with an empty gas tank.

We were able to prepare the car in time for Bristol, where piston problems convinced me to skip smaller races. I knew if our only engine blew, our season was over.

I placed well in Atlanta, then lured by Paul Sawyer's promise of dollars, I ran at Richmond. Paul, a friend of Joe Weatherly, was a popular promoter, who attracted well-known drivers and drew big crowds. Joe promoted races, too, at Norfolk's Princess Anne Speedway. Due to his own hardships in racing, he had empathy and never let drivers leave hungry, always making sure they were paid.

Alf Knight was another well-liked promoter who ran tracks at Phoenix City, Alabama, Montgomery, and Atlanta. Alf had a short fuse, but if he liked you, he was loyal for life, and he was known for his obsession with driver safety.

172

You didn't have to hunt your money if he made a deal with you and if you were having a hard time, he'd send you home with extra, especially if there was a rainout.

At Richmond, Joe Weatherly won, Ned Jarrett came in second, and I placed third; then we lay low, until the Martinsville "Virginia 500," where I sat on the pole. The Martinsville track was a scorcher. Grandstands were built all around it, and since a train track ran by the backstretch, drivers couldn't get cool air. When Lee Petty's driver, Jim Paschal, collapsed in the pit from the heat, Lee grabbed his helmet and became his relief. It was the first time since his accident I'd seen Lee drive.

The race was a wreck-strewn, slam-bam affair with Fireball Roberts, Junior Johnson, Lee Roy Yarbrough and Larry Frank all hitting the wall. Before it was over, I careened out of control and crashed too. I crashed again in the Darlington 300, tangling with pole sitter Fred Lorenzen. As usual, the elusive Lady in Black held her hand out for me.

The "World 600" was another pain-wracked experience. The track was in better shape, but the G force was so strong, it felt as if your flesh was being torn from your face. I built a pad onto my seat to hold me straight, but didn't put in enough cushioning and although I came in third, was hurting so badly I stayed sore for days. By this time, I had faced the fact that my engine was wearing out and since I couldn't rebuild it, I placed farther and farther behind.

Darlington 500 winner Frank Mundy says a race driver has to be too lazy to work, too much of a coward to steal, and braver than Dick Tracy. Racing is fun, and you can get paid for it. I'd disagree with the work part, and the money. The only thing I knew was work, and it was hard. Making money was difficult too, with so many expenses and dominant

"Frank Mundy (shown above) says a race driver has to be too lazy to work, too much of a coward to steal, and braver than Dick Tracy. Racing is fun, and you can get paid for it. I'd disagree with the work part, and the money. The only thing I knew was work and it was hard. Making money was difficult too." (Courtesy Bruce Craig Racing Photo Archives.)

173

Rex White in a Bill Stroppe Mercury in Daytona, 1964. (Courtesy Motorsports Images and Archives.)

competitors. We barely broke even on maintaining the car. A driver's got a rough groove to follow without factory backing and I was desperate. When Mercury offered me a ride and parts, I snatched it up.

The car was built by Bill Stroppe, head of Ford's Mercury Division race team. Glad to get it, I began work immediately. I adapted it, repainted it in my gold car colors, and prepared for the rest of the season.

There were problems from the start. I had difficulty adjusting to leaf springs instead of coils, and there was too much overhang in back and too little horsepower. Mercury just didn't make a good race car. When we went to Daytona, I felt like I was at the Kentucky Derby riding a mule.

We finally got the car set up well enough for me to place second in Old Bridge, New Jersey, but when we ran at Bridgehampton and Bristol, I trailed behind. At Nashville, Tiny Lund blew an engine, and I hit the oil and went under him. His car caught on fire as mine became airborne and flew into the girl on the racetrack billboard. Fans went into a frenzy, trampling all over each

Top: A 1963 "practice" run at Daytona. "When the season began, we were flying high, but we crashed in a junkyard of dreams." *Bottom:* Daytona 1963. "The 427 gave Chevrolet fans, and me, a new sense of pride, and then GM pulled the rug out from under us. It was hard on me, but it was also hard on the fans." (Both photographs courtesy Motorsports Images and Archives.)

Atlanta, 1963. "The original 427 was called the 'Mystery Engine,' but it wasn't a mystery to me. I put the first one built in Chevrolet's test car." (Courtesy Motorsports Images and Archives.)

other to see what had happened. In spite of the spectacle, Tiny wasn't hurt, and I just got cut on my arm. There were probably more injuries in the stands than on the track, but the media splashed my "Flying Car" on front pages all over America.

At the next Darlington race, numerous drivers dropped out due to engine problems, and spinouts due to "bear grease." Bear grease is an asphalt sealant, applied to the track to preserve its surface. It was good for saving bucks but hard on us, as its texture stays slick while it cures. When it was hot, it smelled so bad it could make you sick. After cars run on it, you get better bite, but there's no traction when it's first put on.

In recent years, at Loudon, New Hampshire, drivers talked of a boycott, and almost rebelled, because of the danger from bear grease. They have trouble there because of the cold, which causes asphalt to crack. The use of bear grease still causes controversy today, especially at Darlington, where I can remember the odor mixed with that of cotton oil, which was supposed to discourage bugs. People say southerners are awfully friendly, but the truth is half the time they're just waving off gnats.

My next race at Hickory came to a halt when I hit the bank on my 56th lap. Hitting a bank is different than hitting a guardrail. If you hit a guardrail, you usually bounce back. Coming around curves, a bank can grab your rear end and flip you.

At Richmond, I led 98 laps before Ned Jarrett passed me. Although I was running with the same old gang, the Mercury was hard to handle and Plymouths and Fords were dominant.

Right before the fall race at Charlotte, Louie and Crawford

Left to right: Ned Jarrett, Fred Lorenzen, and Tiny Lund were three of Rex White's biggest competitors. (Courtesy Motorsports Images and Archives; Ned Jarrett Photo Collection.)

Clements were involved in an automobile accident. Louie was seriously injured and not expected to make it. Hard knocks happen, but this one was bad. I was as close to Louie as a brother. Miraculously, as the days passed, he grew stronger.

I continued to race, going to Bill Stroppe's California shop to prepare for the Riverside "Golden State 400." I sat outside the pole, but didn't finish a lap. There was sand, instead of a guardrail, between the track and spectators, and I spun and stuck.

When the season began, we were flying high, but we crashed in a junkyard of dreams. The 427 gave Chevrolet fans, and me, a new sense of pride, and then GM pulled the rug out from under us. It was hard on me, but it was also hard on the fans.

The original 427 wasn't sold to the public. The version put out had 327 style heads on it, with a straight valve cover. Today, the one we had is called the "Mystery Engine," but it wasn't a mystery to me. I put the first one built in Chevrolet's test car.

177

18

Death and Disappointment
Tragedies On and Off the Track

"Fireball's driving reminded me of the movements of a symphony. He was very graceful and knew where he was all the time on the track. Once, he blew his right rear tire during a race in Atlanta. Whereas most people would have worried about hitting the wall, he glided right into pit row. He was hollering 'Give me a tire,' before his crew could get to him."

HAROLD REEVES (Director, Living Legends
of Auto Racing, Daytona Beach Florida)

In '63, Joe Weatherly won the Championship again, followed by Richard Petty, Fred Lorenzen, Ned Jarrett, and Fireball Roberts. Weatherly's purse was almost $75,000. Lorenzen's third brought in an unheard-of $122,587. NASCAR winnings were growing as fast as the spectators. By the end of the year Louie was on the way to recovery, and we vowed to continue our racing team.

In 1964, I drove a Mercury for Bud Moore at Darlington, Charlotte, and Atlanta. Moore had become one of the most famous mechanics in NASCAR, having prepared cars for Joe Weatherly during the year he won the Championship. He would earn additional fame with Billy Wade, Darel Dieringer, and Tiny Lund. Billy, a Texan nicknamed "Mighty Mite," had been David Pearson's teammate in '63 and Darel, who was often called "Yancy," was from Indianapolis. He'd been a basketball player in high school, switching to racing when he turned nineteen. His face became familiar to most Americans through his Goodyear tire advertisements.

At Darlington, I blew a head gasket, as the Lady in Black got me again, and I remember the Charlotte race as if it were yesterday. Jimmy Pardue sat on the pole, with Junior Johnson the fastest qualifier, and I had determined the race would come down to a battle of tires.

Good tires had become more important with the coming of asphalt, and were critical on the new super speedway. Firestone built a really competitive tire in '59, giving it an edge over Goodyear for three to four years. Nothing could equal the sound when those tires popped. There'd be a bang when the tire first blew, then a boom as the car hit the wall. The noise could be heard above the roar of the engines, and fans would jump to their feet to see who had wrecked.

When Fireball Roberts had won the Darlington 500, running for Paul McDuffie, he didn't have the fastest car, he had good tire strategy. Back then, our goal wasn't to run the fastest, it was to guess how fast to run on our right-side tires. If we could go for 100 miles, we avoided a pit stop. I'd worked with my car until it was handling well, and I chose to run Firestone.

By the end of the sixth lap, nine drivers were already out. During the seventh Ned Jarrett and Junior Johnson spun. Fireball quickly followed, his car hitting the wall. The impact burst the fire wall, and flipped his car upside down with fuel spilling into it. It burst into flames with Fireball inside. Ned jumped from his car, which was also in flames, and ran to pull Fireball out but by the time he reached him, Fireball was already badly burned. The grandstands were in an uproar as frenzied fans were barred from trying to help.

Fireball didn't have a chance. He was dressed in a tee shirt and khaki pants because he was allergic to the boric acid fire retardant used on uniforms, and since he'd only run seven laps, his gas tank was full. I continued to race, unaware of how serious his wreck was. Half of the cars had crashed or had mechanical problems.

We ran out of White Dots, which was the tire compound we used, and without my knowing it, the pit crew changed to hard tires. Driving became more difficult but I thought I was tired. I was getting crossed up in the corners and sliding sideways. Over-compensating, I spun and it cost me the race. Jim Paschal took first, Richard Petty second, and I came in third. Despite the spin, it was my best Bud Moore Mercury finish.

I thought Fireball would be all right and went to the hospital, where I found him burned all over his body, but in good spirits. He lived six weeks before pneumonia took him away. Racing lost a champion, and I lost a friend. We shared close to 100 races and 10 years of memories, and Fireball is still the subject of old racing tales.

Once, Fireball was going into a motel parking lot when, forgetting he was on gravel, he put the car in a spin. It spun all right, into the motel and out the other side. Fireball didn't run all the races. Cautious with money, he looked for ones with high purses and those he could win. He used his '62 Daytona 500 purse to pay cash for a house. One of NASCAR's Top Fifty Drivers, Fireball will always be remembered as racing's first superstar.

We looked toward the Atlanta Dixie 400, with heavy hearts. It'd be our first super speedway race without Fireball in it, but with so many super speedway wins, I was sure he made a fast trip to heaven.

I'd learned how to start at high speed by studying tires and compounds with a stopwatch, and again decided to run on Firestone White Dots. The first lap I could go down in the corner, never lift the throttle and hold it. As the tires began to wear, I'd come out more slowly. When I realized this, I used it to my advantage.

The first time I practiced for the Atlanta race, I went out with my tires cold and ran only two laps, then went back to the pits and parked until qualifying. Exhausted, I took a nap on the car's floorboard waiting out the time, then, ran only two laps so my tires would stay cool. The next morning's newspaper headline read "Fastest Qualifier," above a picture of me asleep in the car. I held that "Fastest One Lap Qualifier" record for three or four years. I also may hold another record, that of the "Living Dead." I picked up a newspaper recently, and read I had died.

The following day we ran the race. By the end I'd made it into the lead, but the engine stalled. Ned Jarrett won and I came in fifth. That was the last time I would run a Grand National. Our money was cut and I lost my ride. Billy Wade and Darel Dieringer got sponsorship while I got the boot. I bought Louie Clements's share of our partnership, and that left me broke.

I thought things couldn't get worse, but they did. I had an apartment beside the south expressway in Atlanta, and was listening to the Riverside race on the radio when my friend Joe Weatherly wrecked. Within a few minutes the sportscaster announced he was dead. I had known Joe since I was with Frankie and he ran "modified," and the news hit me as if I'd been slapped.

I flew to his funeral in Norfolk, Virginia with promoter Alf Knight, flagman Ernie Moore, and NASCAR Competition Director Pat Purcell. Coming back we flew into a storm so violent we couldn't see and had to depend on instruments. We stopped to spend the night in Charlotte and went out to a restaurant to eat. Ernie, Alf, and I began discussing the Trenton race in which Purcell barred Frankie Schneider from NASCAR. Words, fueled by alcohol, almost led to a violent fight between Alf and Pat.

During the winter, I got a job building two Chevelles to run in Mexico's Coast-To-Coast Cross Country race. I built the running gear and shipped the parts to Mexico, then flew to Mexico City, taking Jim Delaney and Ken Miller with me. It was my first visit and I was amazed at the city's altitude, and fell in love with the food. Afraid of developing "Montezuma's revenge," I wouldn't drink water, preferring to quench my thirst with a beer called Dos Equis. I still like that beer and drink it with chips and salsa at El Ranchero's restaurant, today.

We had engine trouble from the start. My car went out the first day and the other driver, Billy Wade, didn't make it through the second. When he hadn't cleared the checkpoint, the car's owner, Monty, was sure he'd broken down or wrecked. He decided to go look for him and Ken Miller and I went with him.

We felt as if we were in an airplane as we rode above the clouds, on a mountain road bordered by cliffs. Prior to the race I'd spent about two months learning the towns and the racecourse. They'd had busloads of people crash off the mountains, and there were no guardrails. The road we were riding on was steep. If you ran off one side, folks tried to save you. If you ran off the other, they just placed a candle to mark the spot.

When we came upon two cows, Monty swerved to avoid them, losing control of the car. I grabbed the wheel, but we ran off the edge, dropping 90 feet to the rocks below. Monty was cut on the leg, Ken on the head. I was caught upside down between the roof and the seat, hurting so badly I couldn't see. The others pushed open the door, but left me in. Unable to move and realizing fuel was all over me, I pleaded until they agreed to pull me out by my feet. The pain was unbearable.

Three hours later, three hunters came, but couldn't figure out how to carry me. I told them to remove the backseat and put me on it. Reaching the road was excruciating. They struggled, climbed, and dug their way up the slope while carrying me. When we finally reached their truck, they put me in the back. Still on the car seat, I tied my belt to the truck to keep from slipping out.

They took us to a little first aid station in Tasco. Monty hired a nurse, who insisted on taping my crippled leg. It took a long time to convince her that the problem was my back, and when I did she just gave me an aspirin.

It was hard to communicate as I couldn't speak Spanish, even to ask for Dos Equis. We were 75 miles from Mexico City at 5 P.M. on a Sunday. To this day, Ken Miller talks about the experience.

Jim Delaney stayed with the car. Ken and Monty went to Mexico City the day we wrecked and I stayed with my Mexican nurse until the next day. That poor hospital was so tiny the whole thing was the size of one room.

Twenty-four hours later I arrived at the hospital in Mexico City, hauled there in someone's old Cadillac. The two doctors treating me told me my back was broken. One wanted to operate, but the one who spoke English suggested a cast. Refusing to be cut, I went with his recommendation.

When the cast was put on, my abdomen was flat. I soon found there was no room for eating and had to have a guy with a saw cut out a place for my stomach.

I stayed in that hospital two weeks, then flew to Atlanta on the floor of an Eastern Airlines plane. When we arrived, I was taken out in a wheelchair, and had to crawl on the pavement from the chair to a taxi.

I insisted the doctor in Atlanta saw my cast off, but then couldn't hold myself up. He persuaded me to put on a brace from my crotch to my neck. It was a corset-like thing that pulled my body together. My injury was painful, but I was fortunate. By the end of the 1964 season, Fireball Roberts, Jimmy Pardue, and Joe Weatherly had all been killed. Through a bizarre series of events, all of my serious injuries in wrecks occurred off the racetrack.

Richard Petty took that year's Championship, making almost $115,000.00. In years to come, he would win Final Point Standings another six times. Carless, I instructed Jim Delaney how to build a 1955 Chevrolet, so I could run Sportsman when my back healed.

When I'm determined to do something, nothing can stop me. In Spring of '65, eight weeks after I got back to Atlanta, I won a 500-lap race at Harris, North Carolina, wearing a brace to help hold me up, and continued to run throughout the '65 season.

It wasn't long before Louie Clements joined me. We expanded our racing business into sales, providing tires and goggles to make more profit. He and I clicked like teenage buddies and we made a good team. We had a lot of fun running races together again, experimenting on different tracks and meeting a wide variety of people. Ralph Earnhardt, Tiny Lund, Bobby Isaacs, Bud Moore (the driver), and Jack Ingram were all without rides and running sportsman that year.

Bobby came from Catawba, North Carolina, and had been the 1958 South Carolina sportsman champion. His big break came from mechanic Ray Nichels, who offered him the chance to drive a Dodge. Fighting his temper was almost as big a battle for him as racing, but he acquired a large fan following. He would eventually win a Winston Cup title and become a member of NASCAR's Top Fifty Driving Legends.

We still had our garage in Spartanburg and a lot of fans and young drivers stopped by. The track became a racing classroom, as guys with less experience watched our moves and copied our cars. They learned a lot from us, like how to make the best use of baling wire, and the importance of duct tape. If something fell loose in a heat race, we'd patch it to run the feature.

One of the first races was held in Augusta, and we arrived hungry. I stopped at the Red Pig Barbecue, parked my car with the Mercury on a trailer behind it, and went inside.

183

Bobby Bates, a young local driver, saw me and after I disappeared, crawled under the trailer to take a look at the car's rear end. He was still under it when I returned.

I yelled for him to get out from under there, grabbed him by the seat of his pants, and drug him out. A current member of the Georgia Automobile Racing Hall of Fame Association, Bobby still remembers how badly I scared him.

The Augusta race was the closest race I ever ran. The flagman said I won it by about an inch, but he used his eyesight, and that's not a camera. I don't remember winning a race, with another car by my side, any closer than that. I liked driving on the Augusta Speedway. It was a nice little paved half-mile track in a good location, where I won many times.

That year, I ran 32 races in Sportsman, winning an astounding 20 of them, and coming in second in 10. We'd usually run Columbia, S.C., on Thursday; Shelby, N.C., on Friday; Augusta, Ga., on Saturday; and Harris, N.C., on Sunday. Sometimes, we alternated with Greenville and Asheville. Making just enough money to get by, we were running for pure enjoyment. We were still struggling but there were many others. I remember a driver taking a car off the showroom floor and turning it into a race car while making payments to GMAC, and I'm sure he wasn't the only one.

In the fifties, some drivers would buy a car from the dealership, take out the headlights and cover their holes, protecting the front end with masking tape. They'd attach a large screen to the radiator to prevent damage, and wrap a belt around the window and doorpost to keep the door closed. After a weekend of racing they'd fix everything back, then, they'd sell the same car the next Monday. Others would use rental cars. Ted Chamberlain was one. He'd race it, and then take it back, to make racing affordable. NASCAR stopped that practice when they begin requiring a full set of roll bars.

Up north, where the tracks weren't usually full, promoters sometimes promised large numbers to increase the crowds. To fill the field, people from the pits would start the race in their tow cars, then usually drop out at the end of lap one.

The year 1965 marked a big stride in NASCAR history with the development of the fuel cell and the check valve, which prevented fuel from spilling when cars flipped over. Firestone's fuel cell replaced traditional gas tanks and Pop Eargle designed the first check valve. He made them in my shop using my equipment. I helped him with the welding and fabricating and he sold them to drivers. If there'd been one in Fireball's car, it could have saved him.

Ned Jarrett was the 1965 Grand National Champion, placing first in Final Point Standings, although he, too, had broken his back, in a multicar crash in

Greenville. Soon, I realized, I'd probably made a mistake. If I'd chased points instead of wins, I might have been champion that year. Two championships could have possibly attracted sponsorship.

At the end of the season Louie went to Arizona to work at the Chevrolet Proving Grounds and I was offered a job with a Plymouth dealership in Georgia. Broke and having no money to race, I accepted. Remembering my father's advice to do everything well, I threw myself into it, having no idea it would turn out so profitable. I won an award for becoming one of the highest-paid service managers in the country, then won another one for selling 1,000 engines to Delta in one order.

When the business closed, I went back on the road, buying a rig and becoming a trucker. Missing the track, I practiced my skills on hairpin curves with twenty-ton loads in the back. My car building skills were converted to truck repair. Later, I went to work for Jones Trucking, where Ed Whitworth, the owner, had become my friend. I stayed with him until I retired at age 71.

Racing was hard on my family. Edith and I grew apart and divorced, but we still keep in touch. My second marriage to Jeannette Adamson ended tragically when she died of illness. My daughter Brenda and I stayed close until she died nine years ago from diabetes.

Although my parents and brother are dead, my sisters, Carolyn and Mae Lynn, survive. We have our old memories, and the old family farm, back in Taylorsville. When I go there to visit, I think of my mother, sitting at her wooden frame and making quilts from her flour sack scraps. That fabric was like a tapestry of our lives, held together by my parents' determination and will. I can still picture my father, in his torn denim coat, beckoning me towards the door as he says, "C'mon, boy."

My father wanted me to be a farmer because farming was all he knew. It had worked for him and he believed it would work for me too. I spent my childhood planning my escape. When I did, I pursued my profession with the same passion for racing he'd had for the land. What I learned from him stayed with me, and guided my racing career. Always pushing my limits, instead of producing crops, I was producing speed.

At age 74, I still hear his voice: "Never say I can't do that. Say I'll try, then do it. Don't talk about what's behind you, say what you're gonna do. If something bad happens, put it out of your mind. You done turned that page over." The vision of him pulling on his jacket, lacing his boots, and heading out into the snow is ingrained in my memory.

Today, when young drivers ask my advice, I repeat his words and add my own. Never give up. Keep working until you have what you want and with willpower you'll make it. Racing is a lot like life. You've got to watch your

185

moves and prepare a good strategy. A lot of pain can be prevented by planning.

Should I have stayed in racing? That's a question that can never be answered. Eventually, I would have found another sponsorship. But none of us can say what could have happened. I could have won another Championship, or died on the track. Second-guessing doesn't change or make anything better, and my life has been good. What I didn't expect was that racing would tap me on my shoulder and propel me onto the fast-track again.

19

Motorsport as Megasport
The #2 Sport in the Country

"The most amazing thing in racing has been the increase in fan attendance and money. It has even amazed NASCAR. Nobody ever thought it would grow as big as it is today. I don't see any end to it as long as they make such a show. They not only take in dollars from fans, but from vendors. NASCAR has made big money, but they've also brought big money to drivers."

NED JARRETT (Former ESPN Sportscaster, Member, NASCAR Top Fifty Drivers)

Today, racing's a corporate affair fueled by a hunger for money, glamour and power. While I was racing, NASCAR was changing, but no one could have foreseen its phenomenal growth. It's become the number two sport in America and has over 75 million fans.

In the old days, most fans lived in the Southeast. Today, 60 percent live in other geographical areas. Many of those fans are young and affluent, and 40 percent are women. NASCAR is the most rapidly growing major sport among minorities, with 20 percent of its fan base made up of people of color.

During the time I raced, sports were low-key without much publicity. Radio announcers such as Barney Hall and Bob Montgomery painted vivid pictures with words to involve their audiences, and some boys, hungry for news, used what little was on a sports page to learn how to read.

In the sixties, super speedways set the stage for spectacular speeds, and wrecks lured and increased attendance. Then, when television came to racing, everything changed. The track became a household word.

As media coverage increased, public notice increased, and now people show

"Frank Mundy drove for the Hell Drivers and the Death Dodgers, performing over 2,000 shows." (Courtesy Bruce Craig Racing Photo Archives.)

up in droves. The crowds are so big they baffle me. It's hard to comprehend such a large mass of fans. The tracks have changed, but the infields haven't and they're still a stage for shenanigans.

In the old days, drivers would take a stock car and make it into a race car. Now they take a race car and make it into a stock car. Since today's cars look the same, fans bet on drivers, hooting and hollering, holding pools on their placing and laps. Having worked hard for every penny I saved, I've never been much of a gambler, but when I was driving my rig, I used to stop in Nevada. Using a trick I'd learned from Eddie Skinner, I'd take a ten-dollar bill, get it changed into quarters, and put them all into one slot machine. I'd run the odds up and then see what happened. Whatever came out was what I left with and took home to my daughter Brenda. She loved for me to bring her quarters, even when she was 30. Fans who aren't into betting enjoy other activities, and there are lots of racetrack attractions.

"Racing was, and still is, a demonstration of showmanship. Race fans expect and are willing to pay for a really good show. When I raced, promoters would do almost anything to provide it." (Courtesy Motorsports Images and Archives.)

In the early days, there were bicycle, pedal car, and go-cart races for children. Kids sped down the straightaway and everyone cheered. Stunt drivers put on shows for entertainment, attracting more attention than the race drivers. When Joey Chitwood went around tracks on two wheels and Jake Kochman's "Hell Drivers" provided thrill shows, their antics were far more dangerous than the features.

Frank Mundy drove for the Hell Drivers and the Death Dodgers, performing over 2,000 shows. He learned to drive on two wheels by accident during practice. One night his elbow hit his safety belt release and threw him out of the car, onto the track, and into the path of another stunt car. He is lucky to have lived to tell about it.

One of the more popular entertainers was "Dynamite Bean." During intermission, he'd place a casket in front of the grandstand, climb inside and blow himself up, exciting the crowd into a frenzy.

189

Rex White (left) and Jimmy Mosteller at a 2003 autograph session. "Like me, Jimmy Mosteller claims he was too small to fight and too lazy to run. He was often a race-track mediator, trying to settle things down when there was a conflict." (Courtesy Eddie Samples Photo Collection.)

Racing was and still is a demonstration of showmanship. Race fans expect and are willing to pay for a really good show. When I raced, promoters would do almost anything to provide it.

Once when announcer Jimmy Mosteller was at Boyd Speedway, only 11 cars showed up to race. When the promoter said he was going to cancel the event, Jimmy, a show business expert, suggested he give the drivers a purse in exchange for a show and make his profit from concession sales. The promoter agreed, as did the drivers. One of them, Wildman Jerry Smith, said they didn't all need to be out there, as he could put on an act by himself. When he came out of the number four corner, he flipped the car onto its roof and slid down the straightaway. The car was all torn to heck but the crowd was thrilled.

Some shows occurred without any planning, such as when outhouse holes became nesting areas for bees. At one track, the men's outhouse was down in the pits, but the ladies' was at the number two turn. The race started and the cars dived into the turn. A wheel came off and shot straight into the outhouse, almost knocking it over. Out flew a woman frantically pulling her pants up and pushing her top down. She ran berserk and the crowd went wild.

190

Jimmy Mosteller, who like me, claims he was too small to fight and too lazy to run, was often a racetrack mediator, trying to settle things down when there was a conflict. In the old days, there was no security and if two people fighting weren't separated they'd soon be hurt. Now, security is imperative, not only for fans and participants, but because of our changing world. If there's a fight or commotion, a guard is instantly there. They find protection in police, not hammers and tire irons. We were thankful if there was an ambulance. Now, medics and firefighting equipment are a necessity.

Fans are getting younger and show up days before a race, loading their pockets with freebies from promotional booths and listening to bands. There are contests and autograph sessions, and it's unbelievable what people are selling and what they will buy. Anything with NASCAR on it is a big-ticket item.

Entertainment has also expanded to a much larger scale. I've seen stealth aircraft fly over, parachute jumpers land, and a vehicle drop from a helicopter. Pre-race activities have literally been taken to a higher level.

The super speedways have mascots who drive Legend cars and amaze the crowd with their car tricks. Monkey Wrench in Atlanta and Lug Nut in Charlotte are two examples. They dress in costumes, shake hands with children and kiss pretty girls.

We used to look in the stands to check on the purse. Today, purses, the number of spectators, and media coverage are all guaranteed. It's not unusual for Nextel drivers to make millions of dollars a year. Nextel replaced Winston, and will make NASCAR bigger business, as Winston was limited in marketing due to tobacco advertising restrictions.

I didn't race for profit or fame. I ran for the thrill of it, but no longer can a driver make it on a hip-pocket budget. In the old days, we had friends. Today's drivers have a big bucks sponsor, and a multicar stable. A bank account determines who runs and publicity is everything. Politics is as much a factor as ability.

Shy, and hating the spotlight, I was often too busy to talk to the press. My discomfort led to media avoidance. Today's drivers must be prepared, and willing, to make media appearances.

We built our cars, and knew them better than we did our wives. There was a time when you could insult a man's wife easier than his car. He'd be more insulted if it was his car, because he considered it personal. Drivers today rarely know the men who build their engines.

Jimmie Summerour, a racing mechanic who is known for improvising, once took one of his cars that was wrecked, attached two wreckers to it, and straightened the axle out to race again. Today's cars look alike with little

"The super speedways have mascots who drive legend cars and amaze the crowd with their tricks. Monkey Wrench in Atlanta is an example." (Courtesy Anne Jones Photo Collection.)

difference in brands, and if one wrecks it's simply replaced with another one like it.

There've been changes in body and style, but the theory's the same, and I'm proud to say they're still using some of my innovations. I won the Dixie 400, using part of a Coke can to adjust my shock. Now, drivers can choose from 500 shocks for each race.

We picked up people to help whenever we could. Modern race teams have fully trained members with top-dollar salaries. Working with high-tech equipment and parts, instead of tow bars and trailers, they have two-story eighteen-wheelers that carry their race cars. The trucks are completely equipped, with bathrooms, kitchens and beds. There's no sleeping in cars or bathing in streams, and most drivers fly to races, and stay in high-dollar motor homes.

We had trouble buying tools and parts, often making our own. Now everything's available, and sometimes donated, from manufacturers. In the old days, 90 percent of what we needed we figured out how to make ourselves. Many things weren't yet invented, and we didn't have money for high-priced tools.

192

Rex White's old "car-building" Spartanburg garage still stands (under new owners) today. "We built our cars and knew them better than we did our wives." (Courtesy Anne Jones Photo Collection.)

We'd beg, borrow and loan things, when somebody needed them, even when it might cost us the race. Constantly in each other's garages, we had a code of cooperation in our brotherhood, with parts, labor and advice included.

The best technology Detroit's developed has come from the racetrack, and the biggest changes I've seen have been in safety. The best innovations are the fuel cell and the driver's cage. Drivers in protective cages are encased in sheet metal just for looks. The cage is so protective it's like a body helmet and although deaths and injuries occur, they are much rarer. Cars have improved 200 percent. Safety harnesses and neck braces lessen strain and shock, and there's clear communication between drivers and pit crews when something goes wrong. All drivers have years of experience, some starting as early as five. They start with go-carts, Bandeleros, and Legend cars, racing late models by the age of 13. They're still fussing as much as ever about NASCAR's rules, but the rules that bite you today will help you tomorrow, and may save your life.

Many of the old tracks are gone, leaving only traces of pavement behind,

"The best technology Detroit's developed has come from the racetrack, and the biggest changes I've seen have been in safety. Wrecks used to be more exciting than the feature." (Courtesy Herman Collins's Photo Collection.)

overgrown with weeds or covered by "progress." The new ones are built mostly the same, with a little more banking or a different groove, but there's nothing special about them. Some drivers are better on one track, some better on all. Some get mad quicker, but most are good speakers.

People ask if racing's a daredevil sport, and my answer is no. It's based on a combination of skills and strategic planning. Some think racing is dangerous and look for big wrecks, but drivers push that from their minds. Compared to laps and miles run, there's less danger in motorsports, than from tailgaters and speeders on highways.

Part of the fascination with racing is the courage of drivers, but conquering fear and testing limits give all people a feeling of power.

There always were and always will be racetrack conflicts, but today they can be high-tech. When races are preempted, fans protest with e-mails. Used by fans, drivers, and owners, computers have chat rooms and racing statistics and they're used to store data, and analyze cars with diagnostic tests. Race radios

194

Rex White (signing, center) during a 2003 autograph session at Atlanta Motor Speedway. (Courtesy Anne Jones Photo Collection.)

are so effective fans can listen to drivers, with every event recorded with a digital camcorder. In the old days, we'd trade a camera, to get a new tire.

Fans used to stand by the track and get covered in dirt, so near they felt wind from the race. They could identify favorite cars, just from their sounds, but today there are so many barriers, fans rarely get close. Everything's seen and heard from a distance.

During the last few years, I continued to receive mail from all over the world, and, occasionally, fans stopped by to visit. Reporters, such as Al Levine, still wrote stories about me, but I had put racing out of my mind because it was past. I was content to live my life incognito, when all of a sudden that changed.

As part of its Fiftieth Anniversary Celebration, NASCAR contacted the most well-known motorsports experts. They were told to select the top 50 drivers best representing NASCAR, who reflected autosport's achievements, as well as its growth. The experts were drivers, crew chiefs, track operators, team owners, writers and broadcasters. They were told to choose drivers from all NASCAR divisions dating from the first NASCAR races held. They were to look for examples of excellence, who'd brought honor to racing.

Top: Rex White (center) with Tom Higgins (left front) and Junior Johnson (right) at the 2002 Moonshine Festival in Dawsonville, Georgia. *Bottom:* Rex White and Bill France, Jr., at the Atlanta Motor Speedway 2002. (Both photographs courtesy Anne Jones Photo Collection.)

Rex White at a recent racing event at Atlanta Motor Speedway. "The people I've met and the places I've been are beyond my dreams." (Courtesy Anne Jones Photo Collection.)

Drivers were separated into five categories:

The Pioneers were the earliest drivers.
The Challengers were super speedway successes.
The Giants were powerful celebrities.
The New Generation were media personalities.
The Future Legends are already making their mark in NASCAR's second half century.

NASCAR President Bill France Jr. said that the "Top Fifty Drivers" made and make NASCAR fans stand on their feet and cheer. He said they were the drivers who made NASCAR history.

I received word that 10 drivers had been selected as members of The Top Fifty Greatest Drivers, in the category of Pioneers. The list was made up of hard chargers including Red Byron, Buck Baker, Tim Flock, Junior Johnson, Lee Petty, Marshall Teague, Herb Thomas, Curtis Turner, Bob Welborn, …and me. I was shocked and astounded. It was the greatest honor I've ever received.

Top: Rex White, during an interview by WSB radio personality "Captain" Herb Emory at Atlanta Motor Speedway. *Bottom:* Grand Marshall Rex White peeks at the crowd from his perch in a 1925 Model T in the Hampton, Georgia, 2003 parade with Anne and Sidney Jones. (Both photographs courtesy Anne Jones Photo Collection.)

Rex White with Richard Petty at a 2003 racing event. (Courtesy Anne Jones Photo Collection.)

My fan mail increased, immediately, with invitations for guest appearances. Sports writers wrote articles and radio and television hosts asked for interviews. Everywhere I go, I'm asked about old times in racing.

At first, I was too embarrassed to get involved, but with the support of my friends, soon found I enjoyed it. There were more and more articles published, and appearances at racing events. I've been in parades, and led one, as Grand Marshall for the city of Hampton. I was inducted in the Hall of Fame in Darlington and Georgia Automobile Racing Hall of Fame Association in Dawsonville, Georgia, have donated memorabilia to racing museums, and have even been "sculptured."

My life changed in an instant, and it has been fun. It seems my past has been fast-forwarded into my future. The people I've met and places I've been are beyond my dreams. I only wish Louie and Bill could share it with me.

Louie Clements and Bill Steel are dead, but Slick is alive, and we attend many driver reunions. I talk to Satch now and then, and still reminisce with old rivals. Frankie Schneider, Junior Johnson, Ned Jarrett, Richard Petty, Marvin Panch, Cotton Owens, and David Pearson are just some of the veterans I

Rex (nearest curtain) attends a Raceway Ministries Bible Study meeting at the Atlanta Motor Speedway. (Courtesy Atlanta Motor Speedway.)

see. Bonded forever by our wars on the track, we share stories of the past, and our sense of community.

I've joined several racing clubs, including Living Legends of Auto Racing, based out of Florida, and the Georgia Automobile Racing Hall of Fame (GARHOFA). Both are dedicated to saving racing memories and have hundreds of members.

Many early drivers in these clubs have become good businessmen, and I believe it's because of the training they learned on the racetrack. Although I went into racing because of the thrill of it, motorsports became my livelihood, and involved many decisions common to entrepreneurs. I first followed my interest, then assessed my skills. I had to learn to get along with people and be willing to travel. To race, you had to have physical and emotional strength, and a willingness to work long hours. You also had to have knowledge. Understanding physics, aerodynamics, and science was essential, although I learned through self-education.

200

I'm retired and at 74, I go everywhere, from large-scale racing events to Bible studies. A firm believer in God, I know he controls the big track, with more power, and more mystery, than the 427. One of my best friends is the Reverend Bill Brannon, a chaplain with Atlanta Motor Speedway's Raceway Ministries, who's also a preacher at Fellowship Baptist. After rarely going since I was a child, I've joined his church, and enjoy the warmth and the friends I've found there.

Left to right: Rex White with Raceway Ministries' Founder Frank Stark and Raceway Ministries' Chaplain Bill Brannon. (Courtesy Anne Jones Photo Collection.)

One of them, Jack Turner, attended races for years, as one of those hard-drinking fans up in the stands. Drawn to God through the work of Bill Brannon and Raceway Ministries founder Frank Stark, he says, "The Lord knew I'd loved racing over 60 years. When I was saved, he gave me a pastor who loved racing too. Now is that a good Lord or what?"

Brother Bill and Jack count themselves as both friends and fans, and we go to a lot of places together, including the speedway. I can still look at a driver's car and tell when he's loose and when he's pushing, and what he needs to have done to it.

I breathe deeply when I go to the tracks, inhaling the smells of hot dogs and grease mixed with burning exhaust. I listen for motors to catch, the different sounds of the cars, and the screaming of spectators. The overwhelming heat of a 500 lapper, the rushing, unrelenting push of racing schedules, the fierce vibrations and g-force pull of the track, and all-night work have lost their appeal. But, I still have the yearning to race, and could set up a car to do well, even today. I miss the revving of the engines, the love-hate relationships with old competitors, the grip of the wheel beneath my hands, the feel of the car on the track, and my 1962 number 4 Chevrolet.

At home, when I'm almost asleep, I think I hear the old '40 Fords, the sound of moonshiners coming around curves in front of our house. The noise begins as a hum and grows to a roar, a throbbing rolling thunder, echoing through my mind and through my heart.

201

Epilogue: Gold Thunder

A Moment Frozen in Time
by Larry Hinson

"If Richard Petty is the Babe Ruth of stock car racing, then Rex White is Joe Di Maggio. Rex did not always have the fastest car, but he could set one up better than most. He had all sorts of contorted positions, and the cars looked different, but he won."

DOUG ALLAN (Publisher, *Motorsport America*)

October 28, 1962.
The last race of the 1962 season on the Grand National Stock Car Circuit.

To this day, I remember the sound of the engine from the Rex White Gold
Chevrolet,
a throaty, roaring, thunderous howl like no other on the speedway.

"Little Rex White" was leading with a handful of laps to go, almost home to
the finish,
breaking free from the growling cars behind him.

But now there is worry, a contagious fear spreading throughout the Chevrolet crowd.
Will he make it?

He hasn't pitted.
His crew chief, Louie Clements, signals frantically for him to get fuel.
The Gold Chevrolet, almost out of gas, is running on fumes.

203

We can hear a change in sound as Rex feathers back on the throttle.

On our feet, and tense with unspoken emotion, we strain to see, the muscles in our necks stretched so far they feel they will tear. We mustn't lose sight of him, mustn't risk missing this last dash for power.

"Go, Go, Go," we shout in unison, our fingers crossed, our hearts beating fast, as the Gold Chevrolet races past us, catching the light of the sun.

"Is he gonna make it?" "You know damn right he is," I answer, consumed with faith, praying my answer will help determine the outcome.

The powerful 409 engine sucks for every drop of fuel it can find as Rex zooms across the finish line with one lap to go.

The car is glistening in the heat and the sun, creating a mist of Gold Thunder as it roars past us.

It's off turn two and then down the backstretch. Thousands of fans stand and scream as #4 races by.

This has been a long time coming.

Please almighty don't let us down now.

Our eyes are riveted on the car as it

swoops off turn four,

down the front chute, and

under the checkered flag.

We won!
Can you believe it?
Thank you Rex White.
Thank you Chevrolet.
Thank you God.
Man, we've made some believers today.

On our way home, our throats, parched and sore, are too hoarse from all our shouting for us to speak.

We sit in silence, bound in brotherhood by words unspoken

—Larry Hinson

204

Appendix:
Rex White's
Career Statistics

- 1960 Grand National (Winston Cup/Nextel) Championship—finishing nearly 4,000 points ahead of second place winner Richard Petty. He scored six wins and thirty-five top tens in racing that year.
- 28 wins
- 110 Top Five
- 233 races entered
- 66 races led
- 36,674 miles completed
- 36 poles
- 163 Top Ten
- 48,367 laps completed
- 4,583 laps led
- Number 4 in all time finishing position in NASCAR Winston Cup history (8.983 average). Ran outside of the top ten only 30 percent of the time.
- Most Popular Driver (1960)
- Stock Car Driver of the Year (1960)
- *Motor Life*'s 1961 "Man of the Year" Award
- Member NASCAR's Top Fifty Greatest Drivers
- Two-time driver for Chevrolet

- Living Legends of Auto Racing Pioneer Racing Award
- National Motorsports Press Association Hall of Fame
- Georgia Automobile Racing Hall of Fame
- Career Span: 1954–1965
- Total NASCAR career earnings: $223,514.00
- Smokey Yunick Pioneer Award

Index

Index

Wilson, Guy 94
Wins 205
Winston Cup 3, 35, 67, 95,
   126, 183, 191, 205
Winston-Salem 75, 109, 129
Winton Alexander 10
Wood, Glen 61, 128, 129, 132,
   141, 142, 150, 164, 165,
   166

Wood, Leonard 128, 142, 150,
   164, 165, 166
Woody Woodpecker 82
World of Speed 122
World War II 17
Wright, Bob 27
WSB Radio 198

Yadkin County 90

Yadkinville, North Carolina 77,
   90
Yankee 500 156
Yarborough, Cale 67, 152
Yarbrough, Lee Roy 164, 173
Yates, Doug 128
Young, Feron 167
Yunick, Smokey 31, 73, 165,
   170, 171

214